JUDGE AARON COHN

MEMOIRS OF A
FIRST GENERATION AMERICAN

Lynn Willoughby

ISBN: 1-4392-1552-9
www.booksurge.com

Visit www.amazon.com to order additional copies.

To my beautiful wife, Janet Ann,

& to my"magnificent" children,

Gail Cohn,

Leslie Cohn, &

Jane Cohn Kulbersh.

For you, I have published my memoirs.

TABLE OF CONTENTS

PREFACE

In my long life I have accumulated more good friends than any man deserves. These dear ones have entered my life as fellow tennis players and bar members, Superior Court judges who entrusted me with the administration of the juvenile court, or simply as fellow citizens of Columbus and Athens, Georgia.

I am particularly indebted to a few people who have aided in the writing of this book. First of all, thanks to my steadfast partner, Janet Ann, for her love, support, and inspiration over our now sixty-eight years together (and counting). Mere words cannot express how much I love my children and how thankful I am for their unflagging interest in setting down my life story. Because of them I finally agreed to publish my memoirs as a legacy for the generations who will follow.

My large, extended family, scattered throughout the Southeast, shares my heritage and my love of country, and I want you to know how much I cherish our special bond. My extended family also includes the wonderful people who work with me in the court system together with our close family employees who have meant so much to me over the years. It is impossible to name each one of you, but you know who you are, and with all my heart, I thank you for your care and trust.

Thanks to Marilyn Hirsch for loaning photographs of my grandparents. Regina Satlof Block's excellent research on my family's roots also has been invaluable. So was the fine war diary of my hero, the late General James H. Polk. His children Jody and Jamie (along with their spouses Jonathan and Mary) are as dear to me as my own children, and I thank them for their enthusiastic support of this biography as well as for permission to quote from their father's book.

Lastly, thanks to the charming and professional Lynn Willoughby for crafting the story of my life. Over the past year, our relationship has become more than a business arrangement. The Cohn family now considers her to be one of our own.

INTRODUCTION

"If any person is allowed to be persecuted, we are
no longer a free nation. If we allow any group to be
persecuted, it is a breach in the fiber of democracy."
Aaron Cohn, quoted in *Columbus Ledger-
Enquirer*, May 7, 1983

The life story of Aaron Cohn is a thoroughly American story.
His Russian Jewish parents immigrated to this country before
World War I to escape religious persecution. Although they
encountered social prejudice in their adopted land, the Cohns
thanked God everyday for the opportunity to live in a country
where their property and their basic freedoms were protected. Sam
and Etta Cohn instilled in their son Aaron a fervent patriotism
for the nation that had sheltered them from tyranny. To repay the
family's debt to their adopted nation, Etta Cohn expected Aaron
to give back to his community in full measure.

Aaron has lived every day of his life focused on making
good his obligation to America and to his family. He volunteered
for active service in the army before Pearl Harbor and landed on
the beaches of Normandy like so many other American patriots.
During the war he worked as the operations and planning officer
of the 3d Cavalry as it blasted across Europe to overpower the
Nazi army, which had so brutally murdered millions of innocent
civilians, many of them children. Near the conclusion of that
war, he strode through the gates of a Nazi concentration camp
and saw first-hand how lethal bigotry can be.

With that horrific sight burned in his memory, Cohn returned to his home town and worked as a lawyer while donating countless hours of his free time to coach and mentor children, to bring the various faiths together through education of their commonalities, to lead various community improvement efforts, and to represent the underdogs of society in the courtroom. Instead of getting angry and criticizing what was wrong with America, he focused on what was right with it. Then he quietly worked within the system to make both subtle and sizable social changes.

His community called on him to lead the voter registration drive during the tumultuous 1960s civil rights struggles, and when civic leaders saw how he had managed such a political hot potato, they asked even more of him. Just as he was notified he was in the zone of consideration for promotion as a general in the Army Reserves, he made a very difficult decision to retire from military service in order to accept another post that called to him even more—juvenile court judge.

To many people, the juvenile court represented the bottom of the barrel in prestige within the federal justice system, but to Aaron it felt like the mountain top. His love of children and his drive to help the underdog dovetailed into one rewarding and lengthy career, begun in 1965 and continuing to this day.

The Honorable Aaron Cohn is today the longest-serving juvenile court judge in America. After forty-three years of service, he still loves his job; he still adores his country. He tells everyone he meets, especially those delinquents who cower before his bench, how lucky they are to be an American.

CHAPTER 1

RUSSIAN ROOTS

Although Aaron Cohn came of age in the dusty streets of Columbus, Georgia, his familial roots extended across the Atlantic Ocean to the chilly Russian provinces of Lithuania and Ukraine. In the late nineteenth century Aaron's parents lived in different regions of the "Pale of Settlement" near the western border of the Russian Empire. There, Jews were encouraged to live, presumably without further discrimination after enduring centuries of mistreatment.

The Jews of the Pale of Settlement had the benefit of living among the largest Jewish population in the world. Their concentrated numbers allowed their culture to flourish; yet even here the Jewish people suffered persecution, and over time their plight worsened. Aaron's parents' families decided their best hope lay in immigrating to America. They met each other in a typical southern town in southwest Georgia as they began their lives anew—a life vastly different than anything they had known.

Aaron Mednikopff (Aaron Cohn's maternal great grandfather) had lived in Kiev, a key industrial center in the Ukraine and the major commercial center of the southwestern reaches of the Russian empire. A man so large he had to stoop to pass through doorways, by anyone's standards he was a success. Although Mednikopff was a Jew, Czar Alexander II had allowed him to own property outside the Jewish sector of Kiev after he had completed his mandatory twenty-five years of service in the Russian army.

In the 1830s Aaron Mednikopff bought an entire city block in the area known as Shulyafka. This property included a two-story building, which housed seed and grain stores and a grocery store on the street level. He rented out the apartments on the second floor and owned other apartments in another large building. Aaron's wife Hannah gave birth to seven children between 1840 and the 1860s. When his children matured, Aaron gave each of them a portion of his property, and they became shopkeepers.

The Mednikopffs' eldest daughter, Minnie, born in 1852, resembled her father in stature. She was a stout red-head, as strong as an ox, and she never shied away from saying what was on her mind. Minnie met her future husband, Moses, after he moved to Kiev from Germany. Moses Block's parents had died when he was a Yeshiva student. After staying with various family members, so poor they could only afford to eat kasha (groats) for dinner, Moses's maternal grandparents in Kiev sent for him when he was thirteen. The Hirsches proudly adopted this bright, young man who could speak seven languages and was a Talmudic scholar, and Moses gratefully took their name.

Bowing to Russian law, which required all males to serve in the army for twenty-five years, Moses became a soldier in the 1860s. Because he was a Jew, he was not permitted to rise above the rank of corporal, but his sergeant often ordered him to report to the colonel so he could write letters for him. Over his years of service, he and the colonel became good friends, yet an invisible line of prejudice divided them.

After Moses married Minnie, Aaron Mednikopff gave the couple a grain and feed business. Minnie insisted that she run the store so that Moses could continue his religious studies. While she lugged heavy grain and flour sacks on her back with the strength of a man, Moses pored over Hebrew texts and became a binder of fine, leather books.

But when a bomb killed Czar Alexander II in March

Minnie Mednikopff Hirsch,
Aaron's maternal grandmother,
was born in Kiev.

1881, the happy life that Moses and Minnie Hirsch had shared in Kiev abruptly ended. Many Russians blamed the Jews for the Czar's murder, and even though this was far from true, a wave of retaliatory anti-Jewish riots swept over the Pale of Settlement. These "pogroms" would continue for three horrific years while the government turned a blind eye to the destruction of Jewish homes, businesses, and synagogues.

Before this wave of pogroms ended in 1884, thousands of Jews lost their homes and were reduced to poverty. Then, blaming the victims for the violence set against them, Czar Alexander III instituted the May Laws in 1882. These edicts legalized a

Moses Block Hirsch, a Talmudic scholar, immigrated to America with his family to escape the Russian pogroms.

"systematic policy of discrimination" against the Jewish people, confining them to urban areas and instituting strict quotas on the number allowed to go on to secondary and higher education or to work in one of the professions.

The Jewish people began to reevaluate whether they could ever be successful or secure in Eastern Europe. Thus began an exodus of more than two million Jews, who fled mostly to America and the United Kingdom.

In this mass emigration of the 1880s, Minnie Hirsch's sister, Bella Bonfeld, arrived in America, settling first in Birmingham, Alabama, where other Bonfeld family members lived, and then moving to the sleepy town of Columbus, Georgia, by 1896. The Bonfelds opened a clothing store at Twelfth and Broad Streets and lived in an apartment over the store. With hard work they began to prosper.

Meanwhile in Russia, Moses and Minnie Hirsch hoped for the best and focused on raising their growing family. Their daughter Etta was born in 1888, and by 1899 the family numbered ten.

But in 1903 an even bloodier wave of pogroms broke out. This time two thousand Jews died defending themselves and their property. Soon after Moses and Minnie's daughter Rebecca married Boris Satlof, these newlyweds joined the Bonfelds in Columbus in 1904, taking with them Boris's brother Charles.

Once in America, the Satlofs read the terrifying headlines that Cossacks had again swept through Kiev. Although Rebecca would not learn for months that her family had survived, the Hirsches had lived through these 1906 attacks because caring Christian neighbors locked them in their own barn. As the Hirsch family hid in their hayloft for three days, every overheard scream felt like a knife in their own hearts.

Finally, after the Czar's horsemen moved on, the Hirsches peeked outside. Young Etta thought at first it had snowed, but the white fluffy substance littering the ground was actually a storm of feathers released from slashed quilts, pillows, and mattresses, where the army had hoped to find hidden treasure. Except for the clothes they wore, the Hirsches had lost everything.

Worried sick about her family, Rebecca Satlof wrote her parents. "If you are still alive, come to America. Whatever we eat, you will eat."

When Moses received his daughter's letter, he was at last ready to leave his homeland to begin a new life on alien soil. Forgiving most of the debts his customers owed him, he collected just enough money to pay for passports and passages for himself,

Minnie, and four of their children: Rosa, Etta, Ruby, and Joseph, plus a niece, Runya Mednikopff. (Three other children would join them later in America.)

On January 1, 1906, the Hirsches boarded a train for the port city of Bremen, Germany. While they waited a week for the next American-bound ship to enter port, someone stole fifty precious dollars from Minnie. With just enough cash remaining to reach their destination, the family embarked on a three-week voyage to America.

The rough Atlantic crossing seemed interminable as they traveled in steerage (third) class. The stale air below decks reeked of sickness and sweat. Eighteen-year-old Etta was ill throughout the entire voyage. Only when their quarters were being cleaned did the Hirsches have a chance to climb the stairs and stand on deck where they could breathe in the fresh, salt air, but Etta was relieved to be led back to her bunk where she could lie down again. The day she at last spied the shoreline of Maryland she began feeling better, and when they docked at the Baltimore wharves she was grateful to step onto solid ground again. But having crossed the broad Atlantic Ocean, their travels were still far from over.

The Bonfelds, who sponsored them, arranged for someone to meet them at the ship, then feed, bathe, and comfort them before they boarded a train for Columbus, Georgia. After three days of traveling down the Atlantic Seaboard and across Georgia, they arrived at the Columbus train terminal on Sixth Avenue in the dead of night. When they stepped out of the red brick station into the darkness, they were surprised to see so few city lights and no tall buildings. Kiev had been so brightly lit at night that "you could find a needle" on the sidewalks.

"Where's the city?" Etta asked nervously.

Moving from the metropolis of Kiev to a town the size of Columbus was going to take some getting used to. But here they were relatively safe and free to pursue a new livelihood of their choosing. The Hirsches moved in with Rebecca and Boris Satlof, and Moses began peddling, but this occupation did not suit him.

People called him Santa Claus because of his long beard, and the language barrier prevented the natives from understanding him. At the age of sixty-one, it was a challenge for Moses to learn yet another language. Moses and Minnie sent Etta to live with her Bonfeld cousins in Pratt City, Alabama, cousins while she learned English.

After five months with the Satlofs, Moses and Minnie moved out to open a grocery store on the corner of Sixth Street and Second Avenue and live in rooms behind the store. Etta returned from Alabama armed with a fluency in English, which would be a great help to her parents. Within a few more years, they moved their business to a prime location on the northeast corner of Ninth Street and Fourth Avenue alongside the railroad tracks. They sold, among other things, kosher foods that they ordered from Atlanta.

The store became a community gathering place. When other recent immigrants walked in, they found kind, gentle Moses sitting by the wood stove reading the Talmud. They relied on him to write and read their letters from the old country. Meanwhile daughters Rosa and Runya contributed to the family income by making lovely hats and dresses for the Bonfeld store until it closed in 1910 when the cousins moved to Boston.

As the Hirsch girls came of age, they found husbands in Columbus. Daughter Rosa married her sister's brother-in-law, Charles Satlof, whom she'd known as a child in Kiev. Ruby married Dave Cohen who ran the kosher meat market. Etta met Sam Cohn who was a recent arrival himself from Kovno, Lithuania.

The Hirsches continued to work hard and slowly prosper, but they were by no means wealthy in 1912 when Minnie and Moses's granddaughters arrived from Kiev to live with them. The Russian girls burst into tears when they saw their grandparents' home.

"This must be their country cottage," one of them said hopefully.

Moses Hirsch (seated behind table at center stage, wearing dark hat) took part in the ceremony to lay the cornerstone for the synagogue on Seventh Street.

At the end of every work week, the Hirsches could be found each Sabbath at a minion, or prayer meeting, in the home of one of the other recent Jewish immigrants. By 1913 the group had enlarged to thirty families, and they built a synagogue near the corner of Seventh Street and First Avenue. With his knowledge of the Talmud, Moses Hirsch became a revered leader in the new synagogue. He was among the leaders who took part in the laying of the cornerstone.

More than just being a place of worship, the synagogue was a community center and a home away from home where Yiddish was the primary language, and services retained the flavor of the Old World. In this supportive community, members closed ranks to support their own. One person's suffering was shared by all.

These synagogue members represented only one segment of the Columbus Jewish population. Those who had arrived several generations before (mostly from Germany) attended Temple Israel. Organized in 1854 as B'Nai Israel (meaning "the children of Israel"), the temple's handsome building stood on Ninth Street, a stone's throw from the Hirsch store across Fourth Avenue. Its beauty exemplified the elevated stature of this group within the general community.

Also attending temple services were a cluster of Sephardic Jews. Centuries before, these people had been driven out of Spain and gone on to live in such places as Brazil and elsewhere in Europe before making their way to New York in the seventeenth century and then migrating southward. The most well-known of the Columbus Sephardics was Raphael Moses, who was a brilliant attorney from Charleston. Moses's home, Esquiline, was one of the most beautiful estates in the city. During the Civil War, Moses served as a commissary agent for the Confederacy, and his two sons died fighting for the South. With time, the Moses line of descendants died out and with them, the Sephardic Jews of Columbus.

By the 1880s services at Temple Israel had become "reformed." Much of their services was conducted in English instead of Hebrew, and while members of the synagogue wore yarmulkes and prayer shawls, members of the temple dressed more like their Christian counterparts.

More than just apparel divided the people of the temple from the synagogue. Like the Sephardic Jews, the other Jews descending from nineteenth century immigrants to the Old South had fought for the Confederacy and had thoroughly assimilated into the mainstream culture. At the turn of the twentieth century, they did not want to be linked with the newer immigrants whose heavy European accents and folkways set them apart as foreigners. The two groups kept to themselves socially. Even the homes of the newer immigrants were clustered together in a neighborhood bounded by Fourth Avenue, Seventh Street, Second Avenue, and Ninth Street.

In this synagogue neighborhood lived both Etta Hirsch and a boy named Sam Cohn, who had been born in 1887 in Kovno, Lithuania, as the youngest of eight children. Little else is known of his heritage. Even Sam's father's name is lost to history. Sam's mother, Celia Luria Cohn, became a widow not long after her oldest sons, Max and Ephriam (called Frank by the family), left home to escape mandatory service in the Russian army. The brothers surfaced briefly in South Africa in 1902 at the close of the Boer War. There they opened a trading post in the new British colony. By at least 1906 they had moved on, this time to America, where they settled permanently in Columbus, Georgia. Max Cohn became a well-known clothing merchant on Broad Street (sons Sol and Harry would continue this business long after him), and Frank opened a scrap metal business.

Meanwhile back in Lithuania, Max and Frank's father died, leaving Celia Luria with five daughters and a son to rear. Thirteen-year-old Sam began to support his family by trading livestock, but making enough to support a family of seven was a great challenge. Once Frank and Max became established in Columbus, they wrote their baby brother to instruct him to bring their mother and sisters to America. Sam was nineteen years old in 1906, the year he convinced Rhoda, Dora, Rachel, Sarah, and Ethel to pack their few belongings for the United States.

It was harder to convince Celia Luria to leave her homeland. In her middle age, she simply had more to lose, and she would never feel at home anywhere else on Earth. Sam arranged their passage in steerage class from the Baltic seaport on a steamship bound for New York.

Leaving the Pale of Settlement only five months after the Hirsches had emigrated, the Cohns encountered similar conditions on their long ocean crossing to the port of New York—crowded, unsanitary quarters without the benefit of a view of the horizon. But at last they stood on deck to glimpse the exultant Statue of Liberty at the entrance to the harbor with the skyscrapers of New York City beyond it, and nearby the red brick buildings of little Ellis Island where twelve million poor immigrants processed into the country between 1892 and 1954.

Sam Cohn rides near his livery stable on Front Avenue across from the W. C. Bradley Company.

The Cohns would long remember the sights and sounds of their first encounter with their adopted country as they joined the long lines of people filing through the island's federal immigration station. The walls of these imposing buildings reverberated with the melody and cadence of the many different languages spilling into the cavernous rooms.

While wealthy passengers received automatic entry into this country, third class passengers like the Cohns submitted to a six-second physical exam and answered a series of questions about who they were, why they had come, and how much money they had. The Cohns probably spent less than one full day on Ellis

Island before being released to enter the US. Then, boarding a ferry for the mainland, they made their way through the bustling city of New York to a train station where they purchased tickets for far-away Columbus, Georgia.

Sam and the women he accompanied arrived in Columbus lacking money and a fluency in the English language. They would learn to adjust to eating unfamiliar foods and living in a hot, humid climate. They would also learn how to assimilate into this provincial southern culture where Jews were in the distinct minority.

While her children acculturated easily, Celia Luria Cohn refused to give up her Old World ways. She never learned to speak English, and because of abuses in her past, she feared Christians, especially boys, until the day she died. Her children and her synagogue became her new homeland as she exiled herself from Columbus's Christian society.

Never having had the benefit of school, Sam Cohn could not read, and the only two words he knew how to write were those of his own name. But in Columbus he had the benefit of having two big brothers he could lean on. He also had pluck and an endearing personality, and after all, this was America where dreams come true.

With his brother Frank, Sam collected scrap metal door-to-door. Then the Cohn boys resold it for a profit of a few pennies until, after weeks of hard work, they were able to afford a mule and wagon to enlarge their scrap metal business. Sam purchased supplies at the Hirsch grocery store where Minnie and Moses's daughter Etta, with her diminutive stature and large brown eyes, caught his fancy.

At five feet, five inches, Sam was neither large nor strong, but he was a natural horse trader. As Sam became more established, he traded one horse for another and another until he eventually acquired several. It seemed he always got the better end of a deal. The only men who bested him were the gypsies who camped from time to time in the Beallwood neighborhood. Sam loved to visit their camp and drink with them. He enjoyed attending their wakes. He shared with them an appreciation for beautiful horses and a sound intuition for recognizing a superior animal.

With time Sam and his brother Frank decided to split their business. Frank continued to deal in scrap metal as the E. Cohn Scrap Yard, while Sam opened Sam Cohn Livestock Company and began selling horses and mules to farmers. Sam's business developed into a successful enterprise. For fifty years, he was reputed to be fair and honorable in all dealings. His passion for horses enabled him to remember the genealogy and history of each one. Years after he sold an animal he could recall many details about it. For instance he might say, "I bought that mule in Omaha in 1919. He pulled the ice wagon." And if Sam told a buyer that a certain horse could walk, trot, or canter, by golly it could. One could always count on Sam Cohn's word.

Of course, that didn't stop Sam's most loyal customers from telling jokes in which he was cast as a more typical horse trader. One of their favorites involved a buyer who returned to tell Sam he was disappointed in the last animal he'd bought. Sam asked him why, and the man said, "You told me the horse was healthy, but you didn't mention he was blind. When I turned the horse into a pasture with a lone pine tree standing in the middle of it, the horse galloped right into the tree and killed himself."

"Well," conceded Sam, "Perhaps I forgot to tell you that that horse didn't give a damn."

WE ARE NOT RESPONSIBLE FOR DEATH, SICKNESS OR ACCIDENT OF ANIMALS AFTER DELIVERY TO PURCHASER

Columbus, Ga., _____, 194____

M_____

BOUGHT
OF   **SAM COHN**

Dealer In

HORSES, MULES AND WAGONS

Phone 3-7531   1032 Front Ave.

CHAPTER 2

School Days

S am married Etta Hirsch on February 23, 1910, at the International Order of Odd Fellows Hall on the east side of First Avenue between Tenth and Eleventh Streets. The Cohns

first lived in a home on Tenth Street with spacious rooms and a monthly rent of $12.50. Etta became pregnant with Sol soon after their marriage, and pretty little Anne came close behind. As children began to arrive, the Cohns moved into a house diagonally across from her parents' store on the narrow, dirt lane called Fourth Avenue. This house stood right next to Temple Israel, although Sam and Etta never severed their allegiance to the synagogue on Seventh Street after it was built in 1913.

Sam and Etta Cohn, both recent Russian immigrants, met in Columbus, Georgia, and married in 1910.

Sam and Etta's middle child, Aaron, came in 1916 with Sophie following a year behind him and cute, little Harold, the baby of the family, arriving in 1923. Houses along Fourth Avenue were mostly wooden, one-story buildings with deep front yards that were perfect playgrounds for the many neighborhood children. White people lived on the west side of the avenue; black people lived on the east side.

Then the Cohns moved into a second house on that same block (the 800 block). One fearful night, it caught fire while the family was sleeping. If their Christian neighbors had not gotten them out of the house in time, they would have perished. These kind people gave them clothes to wear and helped them start over in their third house on the same block, this one at 809 Fourth Avenue. Sam added a partial second floor to this house so there was room for his sister Ethel (who didn't marry until later in life) and his mother (who lived with them in her declining years). Aaron shared a room with Sol upstairs, right next to his bubbie's. ("Bubbie" was Yiddish for Granny).

It seemed Etta was always downstairs in the kitchen. Aaron loved his mother's pie and chocolate cake. The whole town marveled at Etta's strudel. Their meats were kosher. She called the rabbi to oversee the slaughter of each backyard chicken. Aaron told his mother on these occasions, "I sure do like chicken, but I sure would hate to *be* a chicken."

At mealtime Etta never sat at the dining table with her family. Instead she happily hovered over them, waiting on her husband and children. Only after they were sated did she sit down to eat with her domestic servant.

Living on Fourth Avenue was ideal for Aaron because he could easily keep abreast of what was going on in town. His first childhood memory was the sound of black people walking past his house, balancing baskets of fresh vegetables on their heads, their strong voices hawking their harvest. "Peas! Tomatoes!" they called.

He loved the annual visitation of the Ringling Brothers Circus, which unloaded its boxcars just behind the courthouse on Ninth Street. Aaron and his friends trailed along as elephants, trapeze artists, and clowns spilled into the street and strolled down to erect their tent at the Fourth Street circus grounds,.

But for Aaron, the best thing about living on Fourth Avenue was being able to stand at the edge of his lawn every autumn to await the results of the annual Georgia-Auburn football game, which was played at the neutral site of Columbus's Memorial Stadium from 1916 to 1958. Each year, young Aaron paced the lawn, waiting for the game to end while intermittent roars drifted over to him from the stadium four blocks away. When the game finally ended, the little boy yelled to every passing northbound car "Who beat?" until someone answered him.

If Georgia won, Aaron was happy as a lark. But if his team lost, he was devastated. His mother's response, win or lose, was always the same. "Darling, go wash your hands. Supper is being served." As soon as he was old enough, Aaron found a way to attend the annual Georgia-Auburn games in person.

Aaron was a sweet natured, blue-eyed blonde with freckles sprinkled across his nose. But the boy became a force to be reckoned with on certain occasions. There was nothing sweet about the way he guarded his house. Whenever uninvited people walked in his yard, he threw bricks at them. And occasionally his anger worked against his own best interest, like the time he bought himself a treat of "wax pipes" with the change his mother was expecting him to bring home from the store. When Etta challenged him about where her money was, he showed her the sack of tiny wax bottles with sweet liquid inside. When she reminded him he had promised to return the change, he threw down his sack of treats and stomped on them until they became an oozing mess.

However, Aaron was usually not in such a devilish mood, and he learned much about comportment from his mother, who never said an unkind word about anyone. Etta was not the sort to ever kvetch. But she did worry about what would become of her children. She was always saying to Aaron, "Son, promise me you won't become president of the United States." She didn't want him to live with such a burden.

With a tinge of exasperation in his voice, Aaron always reassured her. "I raise my right hand to God, Mother. I will never run for president."

To Aaron, his mother was the embodiment of an angel. She never raised her voice. Her children merely received "a look" that was usually sufficient to convince them to reform. When she did scold them, she did so by saying, "What will our neighbors think of us?"

From his mother's concern about the family's reputation in the community, Aaron learned that as a member of a minority, what people thought of you was more important than it might have been to someone in the dominant culture. Embarrassing the family was something to be avoided at all costs. Aaron understood early that one's reputation was his most precious possession.

For the most part, Etta maintained a placid demeanor and overlooked many of the social snubs that routinely came to her because she was Jewish. The only thing that regularly disturbed Etta's serenity was a recurring nightmare. In it, she tugged at her father's sleeve as he led her back to Russia. She begged him to stay, but if he had to go, she pleaded with him to leave her back in America. When Etta awoke from this dream, she was always flooded with relief to find herself safe and sound in Columbus.

Sweet natured Etta Cohn adored her family and her adopted nation.

She loved her adopted home town with a fervor that natives could not appreciate. She continually patted young Aaron on the head, asking him, "Do you know how lucky we are to be Americans?" Etta would never return to Russia, not even for a visit. As far as she was concerned, her homeland was America, and she could not be happier about that fact. Her husband Sam shared her feelings. To be an American was an honor indeed.

Aaron's extended family in Columbus seemed a nation unto itself at times. It included twenty first cousins and twenty-six aunts and uncles. With three grandparents living within a block of him, loving arms were always available to enfold him.

Early on, Aaron noticed a difference in temperament between his mother's people and his father's. The Hirsch family tended to be kind and soft-spoken. From them, Aaron learned how to be an honorable citizen and one who led by example. On the other hand, a few of the Cohn relatives could be more disagreeable, even cantankerous. From the strong-willed and often conflicting personalities of his father's extended family, Aaron learned the art of diplomacy. His proclivity as a peacemaker was accentuated by his birth order as the middle child of his own nuclear family and was further strengthened by his natural disposition as a problem solver. All of his life, Aaron would abhor conflict among the people he loved.

Besides growing up in the guardianship of a large extended family, Aaron had the benefit of other synagogue members who acted as quasi-parental figures. Jewish homes dotted the neighborhood between the meeting house on Seventh Street and the railroad tracks on Ninth. Including his family, his synagogue, and his neighbors, there were always watchful eyes to hold him accountable to a high standard of behavior. Together the adults of downtown Columbus wove a powerful web of support for his generation.

The small town atmosphere provided a perfect place to grow up, and horseback was Aaron's preferred means of travel. He often rode his horse down the dirt road of Front Avenue from his father's livery stable to the outskirts of the city limits. By the time he was seven years old, he was riding all the way out to the vicinity of Fort Benning and back.

Aaron rides horses with a friend.

On summer days, he played marbles with the black children living across the street. He threw a baseball around with friends. Even though the Chattahoochee River was only a few blocks away, he only swam in it once. His mother wouldn't allow it, nor would she let him go to Lake Juniper with the "Y" kids. She wanted him safe. She didn't seem to realize that some of his friends were the toughest kids in town. A couple of them were even bound for the state penitentiary.

While the black children in the neighborhood attended Claflin School, the white kids went to the Tenth Street School, located at the corner of Second Avenue and Tenth Street. Young Aaron was a good scholar and an easy playmate. Some of the children he befriended at the Tenth Street School became lifelong chums. These included Elizabeth Spencer Garrard, Fred Schomberg, Louise Norman Key, and Cliff Johnson, who grew up to be a well-known clergyman. Future Hollywood screenwriter Nunnally Johnson also attended his school.

As easy as Aaron found it to get along with many different children, he also understood that he was different from them because of his religion. Being the only Jew in his class, he was the only one who did not celebrate Christmas or go to church on Sundays. When Christian kids repeated the slanders they'd heard their parents say about Jews, he was the only one there to receive them. One boy told Aaron he couldn't play with him anymore because he had killed Christ.

"Me?" Aaron gasped. "I never killed anyone!"

Even so, at school when Aaron sang Christmas carols with the Christian children, his voice was as loud as any of them because he wanted to help them celebrate their holy day. Yet there was always a feeling of being marginalized by the very people he honored. When his brother Sol graduated from Columbus High School, the school yearbook displayed all the class members' photographs in alphabetical order—all except the five Jewish kids whose pictures were relegated to a separate page.

It was important to Aaron to become assimilated into the larger community. He loved being surrounded by all kinds of people, having as many different experiences as possible. He never wanted to live in a bubble of Judaism. While proud of being a Jew, he never wore a Star of David on his arm or did anything else that would cause him to feel set apart from others. As much as he wanted to be accepted into the mainstream, he had no intention of acting small so that others could appear to stand taller.

Aaron was only about ten when he witnessed a moment that seared into his psyche. In the mid-1920s, the Ku Klux Klan revitalized in reaction to a new wave of immigration and the loosening of American morés in the age of the "flapper." Many Christian men believed that wearing the robes of this organization represented a stand for public betterment, but beneath the veneer of civic improvement lay the ugly bedrock of hate. According to the KKK, anyone who was not a "WASP" (a white Anglo Saxon protestant) was a threat to the survival of American society.

Aaron's parents did not speak to him about this or any other movement that involved bigotry, but one day as he was playing in his yard, he looked up to see a parade of white-robed men ride by on horseback. Slowly and silently they marched down the red dirt road, parting the neighborhood between the homes of whites and blacks, Christians and Jews, natives and non-natives. Aaron was too young to understand what the KKK stood for, but something about this pageantry struck fear in his young heart.

Although Aaron never felt ashamed of his ancestry, his roots did compel him to defend himself from time to time. The boys of downtown loved to gather near the synagogue to fight each other. Some of them singled out Aaron as their enemy because he was Jewish. They soon learned that Aaron Cohn was not going to be beaten easily. And after earning their respect, he became their friend.

In the fifth grade, Aaron began attending the Eleventh Street School. School days seemed an endless succession of lessons—first public school, then music lessons, then Aaron hurried on to the synagogue for his last class of the day. There he prepared for his Bar Mitzvah, and he had even more incentive to do well here than at his other studies. The Rumanian Rabbi Jacob Shulman, with his long, red beard, used a sharp stick to poke the boys in the ribs when they misbehaved. Rabbi Jacob Shulman was a strict disciplinarian but an effective teacher.

On his way from Chase Conservatory of Music on Third Avenue to the synagogue each day, enemies lurked. Two tough, older boys waited for Aaron so they could block his way to Hebrew class. When Aaron saw them ahead, he accelerated into an all-out run. Using his trumpet as a battering ram, he never slowed. He broke through the block and did not stop until he reached the synagogue. Mr. George Chase eventually noticed the dings in Aaron's horn.

"What do you *do* with this instrument, Aaron?" he asked.

The boy just shrugged.

Aaron (top row, far right) enjoyed his music lessons at the Chase Conservatory, but often used his trumpet as a battering ram.

After fifteen productive years in America, Sam Cohn was becoming the quintessential American success story when he was naturalized as a US citizen in 1921. When he swore allegiance to America, Sam had never felt prouder.

Sam had commenced business at a rented livery stable on First Avenue near Fourteenth Street. At that time fourteen stables operated in town. Although he was not an aggressive businessman, he attracted patronage by being honest and likeable and by working hard. However, just by being Jewish he caused a few of his competitors to feel threatened by his success. When Aaron was about ten years old, a Christian man charged into Sam's office and punched him right in the face for bettering him in business. Sam came home that evening with a black eye and other bruises. But he never considered pressing charges against the man. He only wanted peace.

Even with the handicap of being a member of a minority, by 1925 Sam had become successful enough to build a new, brick home at 831 Second Avenue at the cost of $28,000. This move of merely three blocks brought the Cohns "uptown" from their more humble beginnings "downtown." Aaron loved the location of his new home. Less than fifty yards away stood the imposing 1895 Muscogee County Courthouse. On the courthouse lawn there was plenty of room for pick-up ball games with friends like Bill Hartman, who lived just around the corner from Aaron on Ninth Street. Hartman was a few years from becoming a professional player for the Washington Redskins.

Inside the grand courthouse building Aaron loved to climb the gracious stairs to the second floor courtroom. He was fascinated by the way the attorneys fought each other as fiercely as prize fighters while court was in session, then adjourned to eat lunch together at Spano's Restaurant down the street as convivially as though they were the best of friends. Their example taught Aaron that competition was at its best when it was both fierce and friendly.

Etta Cohn hoped Aaron would become a physician, and from the time he was seven she asked him often, "Wouldn't you like to be a doctor when you grow up?" After all, saving lives was a tenet of the Jewish faith.

But Aaron couldn't stand the sight of blood. He always replied, "No, Mama. I want to be a lawyer."

Then Etta would say, "Well, how about becoming a pharmacist? That would be a helping profession."

"No," Aaron answered. "I want to be a lawyer. And if I can't make a living at it, you'll always feed me, won't you, Mama?"

Aaron was nine years old when the family moved to 831 Second Avenue in 1925. That was the year his grandmother Minnie died. Four years later, Aaron would also lose his grandfather, Moses Hirsch. On his tombstone the family inscribed the adjectives they had often heard people use when describing him. He had been a "pure and upright" man.

In their spacious, new, brick home on Second Avenue, the Cohns had a special room where the children were expected to practice music. Sol and Sophie played the violin; Harold played the saxophone; Anne played the piano. Aaron started with the melophone and graduated to the trumpet.

Sitting on benches that lined the four walls, Aaron and his siblings made a joyful noise. They were not the only Cohn family members to practice together. In fact, Max Cohn's four children formed a family band—the first pep band to play at Columbus High School's football games.

The Cohns' new house also contained a room set aside for the observance of Passover and other holidays. Etta practiced her religion faithfully, strictly following her faith's dietary laws, never mixing meat dishes with milk dishes, etc. As strong as her convictions were, she never sought to impose them on her family. Aaron thought nothing of eating hot dogs or anything else he wanted, and his mother never made him feel guilty for it. Her husband was not religious, and she never pushed him to conform. Sam attended synagogue rarely except on the high holy days. In fact, on the Day of Atonement when the faithful were required to fast, Sam would go to service, then ask Aaron if he'd eaten.

"Let's get out of here and get something to eat!" he would say.

Growing up Jewish in a Christian world fueled Aaron's competitive nature. Being Jewish also helped him learn to judge people by their merit instead of their religion. The Young Men's Christian Association (YMCA) gave him a chance to develop in both these respects. Two blocks away from the Cohns' new Second Avenue home stood the gleaming marble YMCA building. Beside it two clay tennis courts baked in the South Georgia sun. As far as Aaron was concerned, this patch of sunshine was the center of his universe. The only disadvantage he ever found to playing tennis at the Y was the nightly bath required to wash that red, Georgia clay from his feet.

Almost every day, Aaron measured his height with a pencil mark on the wall in his home's upstairs hall, but his slash marks did not keep pace with other boys his age. Even when he graduated from high school, he weighed only 106 pounds. With no Little League in Columbus in those days and no baseball team at

In 1933 Aaron (top row on left) won the state YMCA singles table tennis championship and met Dan MaGill.

Columbus High School, Aaron channeled his love of sports into tennis. In the 1920s Aaron and other boys from his synagogue joined the "Y," the center of all Columbus sports. Director Bob Eubanks welcomed everyone and made no distinction among them. But as a member of a minority, Aaron felt added pressure to excel there.

Every Saturday, Aaron rushed over to the courts to help the janitor roll and line the clay hardpan for the day's competition. Since the adults played in the afternoons, Aaron did not want to waste a moment, and by lining the courts, he was assured of being first in line to play. There was no coach to teach the boys technique so Aaron developed his own style. At his size, he used finesse to beat his more powerful opponents. He became so consistent at the baseline that his competitor usually made a mistake before he did.

His father did not understand why Aaron loved to "chase that little ball around," but the game taught him how to win in other aspects of his life. Tennis taught him tenacity, honesty, and humility. As often as possible, he played boys who were better than he so that he could improve his game. In a few years, he was winning city and state tournaments.

In 1929, the year of the Stock Market Crash and the year Moses Hirsch died, Aaron reached the age of his Bar Mitzvah. After spending years preparing for this moment—weekday

First from left on second row, Aaron was among the 1930 YMCA contest winners.

afternoons learning how to read Hebrew and Sundays taking other lessons, he was now proficient in reading the Torah, the five books of Moses, which contained all the virtues and morals of the Jewish faith. His mother wrote an invitation to all his family members on a plain white postcard. On March 3rd, his thirteenth birthday, Aaron read from the Torah, and the service conveyed upon him the responsibilities of adulthood. Afterward, the family gathered at the Cohn home for a celebratory lunch, and Aaron gave a short speech. When he spoke of how much he adored his parents and how responsible he felt to make them proud of him, his eyes welled with tears.

With the money Aaron received as Bar Mitzvah gifts, he took his father's advice and invested it. His father told him that if he bought a horse for $100, Sam could sell it for him for $150. The railroad cars bringing in Sam's livestock unloaded on Front Avenue, right in front of Sam's stable. Aaron was anxious to see them come in now that he had a monetary interest in the animals. But one of the horses was lying on its back, its feet pointing stiffly skyward, a victim of what the livestock men called "shipping fever."

Sam put one hand on Aaron's shoulder and pointed to the dead animal.

"Tough break, son. That one was yours."

Aaron was crestfallen, speechless. Then it dawned on him that his father was only teasing him.

There's a Jewish joke that goes: "How do

Aaron readies for his Bar Mitzvah.

you keep a kid from going to temple? Celebrate his Bar Mitzvah."
Once Aaron's studies were completed, he had plenty of time for
sports, and he expanded his interests beyond tennis. He showed
a flair for boxing.

On weekends a retired sergeant ran a boxing ring on
Fourth Street, only four blocks from the Cohn home. Crowds
of working class white boys—many of them the sons of textile
workers—gathered to watch locals challenge each other to three-
round fights. Aaron loved to watch these spectacles. One day
when Aaron was about fifteen, a fighter failed to show up for
his match, and before Aaron knew what was happening, people
were pushing him into the ring. Aaron was not interested in the
challenge until he heard someone yell, "Kill that Jew boy!"

Being singled out as an enemy just because of his religion
stung Aaron to the core. He flung himself into the fray with the
fierceness of a bull, and at the end of three rounds, his bloodied
Phenix City opponent hugged him in admiration. Prejudice was
teaching Aaron to be a stronger person than those who rebuked
him. Instead of becoming bitter, Aaron was learning to be
competitive. This quality would serve him well.

As Aaron was growing into manhood, his father was
becoming a business success. In the same year that the Cohns
moved into their new house on Second Avenue, Sam built a new,
brick stable a few blocks away at the corner of Front Avenue
and Eleventh Street, right next to the palatial, antebellum home
of the Pou family. The Pous never complained about having a
mule barn as a neighbor, and the two families were mutually
respectful.

Sam's customers ranged from elite plantation owners to the
poorest of sharecroppers and from the outskirts of Columbus
to the Alabama and Georgia counties of Lee, Russell, Harris,
and Stewart. African American farmers especially loved Sam
and used his stables as their home base when they came to town
on business. They stacked their packages in Sam's office and
walked the uptown streets, buying supplies, conversing with

other farmers, and returning to look over Sam's new stock.

"Kinfolks Corner," a gathering place for day laborers and farmers hoping to catch a ride back across the Chattahoochee River to Alabama, was less than a block away from Sam's stables. On days when it was rumored that a horse breeding or auction would be taking place at the livery stable, workers from the W. C. Bradley Company across the street gathered to watch.

Sam usually carried a riding whip to demonstrate his animals' high spirits, but he nursed a soft spot for poor minorities until the day he died. Sam knew what it felt like to be treated as a second-class citizen, so when down-and-out farmers came to town, Sam would catch them eying the mules, and he would say to them, "Pick out the one you like and take it." When they protested that they did not have money to pay for it, Sam would tell them, "Go make a crop. Then you can pay me."

And if they weren't able to make a crop that year, Sam gave them more time. When a dejected sharecropper came to town from Hurtsboro, Alabama, to return his mule because his crop had failed. Sam, understanding that without that mule the man could not make a crop the coming year either, sent him back home with the mule.

"Just pay me when you can," he said. Ultimately, he forgave many debts.

Many times he did not expect ever to be repaid. When Sam noticed that a poor white man who worked at the Eagle and Phenix Mill was sorely in need of a pair of shoes, he told his son Sol to write a note to Max Cohn, telling Sam's big brother to give this man a good pair of working shoes and send Sam the bill.

Working around a livery stable was as much a part of Aaron's youth as playing tennis. He learned how to ride early, and in high school he began jumping horses. Aaron learned from his father's livestock business that a handshake was a bond. As a matter of honor, a Cohn never went back on a commitment. But when Aaron extended this same code to tennis, Sam did not understand. Once Aaron had set a date for a match, he always showed up. Forfeiting would have been a disgrace to him.

Occasionally Sam needed Aaron to work for him when he had a match scheduled, and Aaron told him he couldn't.

Sam told his son, "You're wasting your time. You'll never get anywhere chasing that ball around." Sam even confided to family members that he feared Aaron would never amount to anything. "All he wants to do is play tennis," he complained.

Aaron graduated from Columbus High School in 1932 at the age of sixteen. His parents thought he was too young to go off to college yet, so he spent the next year working on the Cohn family horse and cattle farm, an acreage leased from the Woolfolk family on Fort Benning Road. On these lovely pastures fronting the Chattahoochee River (which later came to be known as Oxbow Meadows), Aaron helped to tend his father's approximately one hundred head of cattle (cows and hogs) and taught at the Cohn riding academy. On weekends his friends, the five King brothers (Buford, Everett, Edwin, Jack, and Jimmy), came out to ride with him on one of the Cohns' fifteen horses.

Aaron also continued to be a "Y boy." He won the city

This tattered photo of the 1933 YMCA wrestling team features featherweight champion Aaron Cohn, seated second from left.

junior tennis title and the boys' tennis title, and he wrestled with the YMCA's 1933 team. At 118 pounds he won the state championship in the featherweight division. At the age of seventeen, he also won the city table tennis championship in Columbus and the state YMCA table tennis championship in Savannah. Shortly thereafter he won the state Y tennis singles and doubles titles.

CHAPTER 3

Glory, Glory
to Old Georgia

For as long as Aaron could remember, he had planned to attend the University of Georgia so he could train to become a lawyer. Finally, in the fall of 1933, Sam and Etta released Aaron to go to Athens where his brother Sol was already attending college and where Aaron would major in pre-law. Once he left Columbus, Aaron seldom returned home during the school year. He didn't own a car, and the distance was simply too great.

Aaron studies in his fraternity house.

He caught rides to and from Athens with people like Jim Woodruff. To get there from Columbus, they drove through Warm Springs, Greenville, Palmetto, and Fairburn. In Atlanta, they turned right on Spring Street and followed Ponce de Leon Avenue out to Lawrenceville before finally reaching Athens.

There he entered a different world. Being a freshman required some humility. He was required to wear his freshman beanie at all times, and he dutifully donned the red cap with black bill wherever he went. He was sitting with Sol at the Varsity one day when Rabbi Abraham Shusterman walked up to speak to Sol. Sol elbowed his little brother and whispered, "Take your cap off!"

Aaron whisked it off but mumbled, "I thought I wasn't supposed to take it off!" Luckily he hadn't embarrassed himself in front of the fairer sex. Women weren't allowed in the Varsity in the 1930s.

Aaron had less trouble with other freshman regulations, such as the rule that freshmen could not walk under the arch at the front steps to campus. There were no women in any of his classes until he reached law school, and even then, only one of his fellow students was female. Because of her the class would not broach such criminal laws as rape. Discussing that sort of thing just wasn't appropriate in mixed company.

Aaron pledged Alpha Epsilon Pi, one of the three UGA Jewish fraternities. He shared the Victorian style Crain House at 774 Prince Avenue with about eighteen brothers. To reach class from there, Aaron simply stood on Prince Avenue and stuck out his thumb. In a matter of minutes he was riding to the historic, red brick campus, which he had loved from the first moment he arrived. For the rest of his life, nowhere on earth would be as hallowed as this oak-shaded campus.

Aaron ate most of his meals at the fraternity house, but others took advantage of Tony Postero's Restaurant's monthly meal plan, which entitled a diner to three meals a day for thirty dollars. The "in" spot was Costa's, a drug store with a short order grill that also sold ice cream.

Dressed in his cavalry uniform, Aaron stands in front of the Alpha Epsilon Pi house on Prince Avenue in Athens.

In Athens Aaron also had his first taste of Reform Judaism. Services at home had been conducted in ancient Hebrew, but the Congregation Children of Israel used English predominantly. These services seemed more relevant and more vibrant to him. From that time on, he preferred Reform Judaism to the religion of his mother.

At UGA Aaron joined the Reserve Officers Training Corps (ROTC). Ever since he was a child and heard stories of how his Russian forefathers were not allowed to become military officers because of their faith, Aaron had wanted to become an army officer. And when faced with having to choose between serving in the infantry or the cavalry, for him there was no contest. He had grown up on horseback, and if necessary, he would go to war on horseback. He wore his black ROTC uniform proudly, and he was happy to be accepted into the Scabbard and Blade Military Society for those interested in serving in the Cavalry. Before he could be initiated, the society ordered him to stand at attention just inside the door of the girl's dormitory. With his rifle at his shoulder he stood silently for six hours without a word of explanation as to why he was there.

The annual military ball was held in old Woodruff Hall, which was beautifully decorated for the occasion. On the walls high above their heads, the letters of all the campus fraternities glowed softly. The young men, dressed in breeches and spurs, danced with their dates in formal dress to a popular orchestra.

Aaron did not have a lot of money for entertaining his dates. His father sent him $50 each month. Out of this sum he paid the fraternity house $33.50 for room and board, leaving him $16.50 for all other expenses.

Aaron was tapped for the Blue Key Honor Society, and he became vice president of the inter-fraternity council. Future Georgia Governor and US Senator Herman Talmadge was then the council president. He and Aaron became good friends. In dry Clarke County, Herman called at Aaron's fraternity house to play poker armed with a gallon of what he called "mountain whiskey."

Luckily Aaron did not have to study to make good grades. He listened intently to his teachers during class and remembered whatever he needed to know for his exams. The hardest professor on campus was rumored to be the German professor, but Aaron had grown up with the German dialect of Yiddish spoken around him, so he had a head start in learning proper German. He was careful never to use Yiddish in class because this mistake sent the professor into paroxysms of fury in which he threw erasers and banished the dismayed culprit.

Aaron's worst grade came in public speaking. The teacher told him he sounded like he had mush in his mouth. Aaron would not learn how to crisply enunciate his Rs until he served in the army. During the world war, it would be critical for him to be understood over the radio, but until then (and afterward), he retained his soft southern accent.

Not having to study gave him time for sports. Aaron was on the freshman boxing team. He played table tennis at the Athens YMCA with his arch rival, Dan Magill, who was four years younger than Aaron. Aaron had met the youngster when he defeated him at the state YMCA championship in Savannah when Aaron was seventeen. After their match Dan told Aaron, "I hear you're going to the University of Georgia. I live in Athens.

I'll be waiting for you." That was the last time Cohn defeated Magill, who grew up to become the university's head tennis coach and Aaron's life-long champion.

When Aaron first arrived on campus, he was asked which extra curricular activity he would prefer—playing trumpet in the band or playing tennis. Even though his father's voice rang in his ears, saying tennis would get him nowhere, Aaron declared, "I wanna play tennis!"

Aaron (on right) and his tennis partner became state YMCA champs in 1935.

The University of Georgia tennis team played on six new, red clay courts below LeConte Hall. Tennis was a gentleman's sport. There was no coach and no line judge. A player called his own game. Aaron was seeded number one on the freshman team. The next year he was the only sophomore on the varsity team. He and his team won nine of their eleven matches in 1935. In 1937 he played at the number one position and was captain of the team.

This team was not the finest team in the SEC, but it was the smartest. Aaron and several of his teammates maintained Phi Beta Kappa grades, and all of them were on the honor roll. In fact, in his sophomore year the entire team was cited en masse on Honors Day for making the Dean's List.

From 1935 through 1937, Aaron played on the varsity team with people like Ty Cobb Jr. and Igor Cassini. Igor became a syndicated gossip columnist under the pseudonym Cholly Knickerbocker and coined such popular expressions as "the jet set." Igor's brother, the haute couture designer Oleg Cassini, also became Aaron's friend.

Aaron was seeded number one on his freshman tennis team, was the only sophomore on the varsity team, and became captain in 1937.

At the pinnacle of his college career, Aaron was seeded number six in the SEC tournament. He won the university championship in singles, doubles (with Albert Jones), and mixed doubles, and, in his final year in Athens, was captain of the team. Meanwhile he played table tennis at the Athens YMCA and won a state table tennis doubles championship in Atlanta. (The prize was two dozen ping pong balls.)

Going on road trips with his university teammates was the most fun he would ever have. With no coach to accompany them, they simply tossed their wooden rackets into the trunk of someone's car and drove to matches at schools like USC, Furman, and Clemson.

The power houses in those days were the University of Miami and Tulane. Playing the latter team "away" ranks as Aaron's most memorable road trip. One year after their match, the manager of the Tulane team gave the Georgia team a tour of the French Quarter while they were still dressed in their white tennis togs. Beauties in evening gowns called down to them from wrought iron balconies, saying, "Hey, college boy! Come up here, and *we'll* give you an education!"

One of the best benefits of playing tennis for UGA was becoming friends with Andy Roddenbery, a medical student who hailed from Macon, Georgia. Besides meeting Andy, tennis also brought Aaron in contact with the five Nazi exchange students enrolled at the university. Adoring tennis, the Germans often walked down to the courts to watch the play. They also tried to tell Aaron about their objections to the Jewish community in Germany, but Aaron let them know quickly that he didn't want to hear any of their propaganda.

In Aaron's senior year Dean of Athletics Herman Stegman summoned Aaron to his office to tell him he was eligible to receive a full scholarship if he would coach the freshman team and assist the varsity team coach. Aaron was overjoyed. He couldn't wait to tell his father that playing tennis was going to save Sam a year's tuition.

But before Aaron could get home with the good news, the football coach resigned, and the new coach, Joel Hunt, insisted that all the school's scholarships go to the football program. The dean regretfully called Aaron back to withdraw his scholarship. Although disappointed, Aaron told him, "Well, I love my school. I'll coach the freshman team and assist the varsity coach without compensation."

By this time, his summer breaks were almost as busy as his academic years. He spent his first two college summers at military camp. Eighty-five cadets of the Cavalry ROTC trained at Fort Oglethorpe in Chattanooga, Tennessee, for six weeks with the Sixth Cavalry (and two weeks' summer camp each year thereafter). The idyllic horse cavalry camp intoxicated the young men. Handsome officers wearing breeches and boots rode over the fields and through the forests, practicing their tactical maneuvers.

Aaron (right) and his fraternity brother Dan Nathan pose for a photo in front of the Cohn house on Second Avenue before leaving for Fort Oglethorpe.

However, the reality was not quite so dreamlike, especially for someone with the riding expertise of Aaron Cohn. The horses they rode were called "remounts," meaning they'd been retired from active duty. One hot, July day, Aaron's horse collapsed under him. It fell flat on its side on the tar road. Luckily he got his leg out of the way before the horse fell on it.

Aaron found that learning to fire a gun at full gallop was not easy. An officer exclaimed after one exercise, "Thank God! Not a horse or a boy lost."

Working with animals taught Aaron how to be a good leader. One took care of others' needs first. When they returned from riding their lathered horses, they groomed their horses first before attending to their equipment so it would be ready for the next engagement. Then they saw to the care of the men who served under them, and only lastly did they address their own needs.

During three of his college summers Aaron also returned to Columbus to clerk pro bono (as was the custom) in the law office of T. L. Bowden. Aaron was thrilled to have a chance to improve his legal skills, but he hated that the job cut into his tennis time. He lugged his racket with him every day to the courthouse law library so he could play as soon as he finished work. This did not please a female juvenile court judge whom everyone called "Miss Polly." One day she called him over to her table and said in no uncertain terms, "The next time you bring a tennis racket into this god-damned library, I'm gonna break this god-damned racket over your god-damned head. You hear?"

Aaron is ready for action at the firing range near Fort Oglethorpe in north Georgia.

"Yes ma'am," replied Aaron.

After that exchange he stashed his racket elsewhere but continued to play tennis at every opportunity. He even played during his lunch hour in the stifling heat of the South Georgia summer and never felt enervated by it.

One day Aaron got a call that filled him with glee. A voice on the other end said he had been in a bad wreck on Thirty-first Street and needed a lawyer.

"I'm a lawyer!" exclaimed Aaron.

He ran to his father's stable and borrowed Sam's car, then sped up Second Avenue. A policeman named Red Burns, whom Aaron had gone to school with, was soon in hot pursuit. Aaron pulled over and shouted to his friend, "I've got my first client!"

"Go ahead!" called Red, waving him on.

But when Aaron got to the railroad tracks at Thirty-first Street, there was no evidence of a collision. A black woman carrying a basket of fruit on her head walked by, and Aaron asked her, "Have you seen a wreck anywhere around here?"

"No," she said, and after driving around the neighborhood for a while and finding nothing, Aaron gave up and returned to Bowden's office. He soon solved the mystery. His buddies John Land and Ed Wohlwender had been playing a joke on him. Bowden was furious when he heard about the prank. His faith in Aaron's ability to become a good attorney was rock solid.

Aaron returned for his final year of law school in the fall of 1937. That year he also accepted a commission in the US Cavalry Reserve as a second lieutenant. In his class were Ernie Vandiver, who became a governor; Bob Jordan, who became a state supreme court justice; and a number of other future congressmen, like Bob Stephens. Half of his class of sixty graduated, and all of these young men looked forward to returning to their home towns, using their law degrees to improve society from the grass roots up.

CHAPTER 4

COURTING

After two years spent earning his associate's degree in pre-law, then three more completing his LLB degree (equivalent to today's JD degree), Aaron graduated in the spring of 1938, leaving behind the city that had become his second home.

Etta and Sam welcomed him back, and Aaron studied for the Bar Exam night and day for two weeks. When it was over he discovered he was one of only two candidates who had passed the examination at the Columbus courthouse that year. Aaron then worked as the associate of George C. Palmer, who later became a Superior Court judge but who already dressed the part. Palmer wore black and gray spats and a long, black coat with grey striped trousers. His white hair gleamed in the sunlight as he rode around town and through the nearby cotton fields in a chauffeured sedan.

Palmer was a fine criminal attorney with an excellent reputation. He warmed to Aaron because the young man seemed genuinely serious about becoming a good attorney. Palmer summoned Aaron to his office, where portraits of Confederate generals lined the walls. He told Aaron he would like to practice with him. Aaron felt honored and accepted on the spot. The young man enjoyed trial work tremendously. Even so, Palmer's formal demeanor caused Aaron to feel a bit out of place in his company.

One day when they were walking down Eleventh Street to lunch, some of Aaron's cronies, yelled to them from the steps of the YMCA across the street.

"Hey, shyster!"

Palmer turned to Aaron and asked, "Do you know those ruffians?"

"No, sir," lied Aaron. "I've never seen them before in my life."

Aaron continued to enjoy his legal work and even gave assistance to his father at this time. Although he was glad to help, Aaron's first legal action on Sam's behalf landed him squarely in the jaws of bigotry once again.

Aaron taught riding lessons at his father's horse and cattle farm on Schatulga Road, Columbus.

For ten to fifteen years prior to 1938, Sam Cohn kept all his livestock on a rented farm on Fort Benning Road across from the Woolfolk Plantation. In 1938 Mr. Woolfolk told Sam he'd have to make other arrangements. Sam found some ideal land on Schatulga Road near the juncture of Macon Road. The owner was a lady whose husband traveled periodically to a

German spa. With her spouse out of the country, the woman's financial advisor (a prominent banker at one of the national banks in Columbus) advised her to sell her land to Sam, which she did. By the time Sam moved his cattle out to the new farm, the husband had returned home. When Sam needed a quitclaim deed to have the boundary lines surveyed, Aaron walked over to the husband's office in the Empire Building to get his signature for Sam's lawyer who was handling the closing.

The man's eyes narrowed as Aaron approached him. Angry his wife had relied on someone else while he was away, he directed his full wrath at Aaron.

"You, God damned Jews! All you people do is cheat people."

Aaron thought, "Same old story. Find a scapegoat to compensate for your own shortcomings."

Even so, it got under his skin, and when the man called Aaron and his family "thieves" Aaron felt like throwing him out of the nearest window. With all the restraint he could muster, he remained calm and did not respond to the abuse. The man threw the signed document at him, and Aaron walked away, comforting himself with the knowledge that he had accomplished his mission even at such a cost.

Another disheartening incident happened at about this same time when Aaron was hired to represent someone. When Aaron told the sheriff, who was a friend of his, that he had been retained, the sheriff told him to expect some trouble with the opposing attorney. Aaron didn't know what he meant, but decided to think positively. He prepared thoroughly and argued his case well. But when the opposing attorney stood up to speak, he pointed the tip of his cane at Aaron's heart and said, "Your honor, that boy doesn't know the law. All he knows is Jew law."

The one place Aaron did not find discrimination was at the YMCA. He played tennis there several times a week and started playing volleyball. Not being as tall as some of his team members, Aaron became the all-state "set-up man." For other social outlets, Aaron renewed acquaintances from his old neighborhood and also made some new friends among the Reform Jewish community.

By the late 1930s twenty years had passed since the final wave of European Jewish immigrants had settled in Columbus, among them Aaron's parents. Up until then, the two Jewish groups had remained isolated from each other. The Reform Jews who attended Temple Israel socialized at the Harmony Club on Macon Road. The Orthodox Jews of the synagogue belonged to the Standard Club, located at the site of the old Muscogee Club on Broad Street and Thirteenth Avenue. But as Aaron's generation—the synagogue's first generation of American-born citizens—reached maturity, both groups were feeling more inclined to mingle. They agreed that their children should have the benefit of a larger circle of friends.

When they formed a youth group, twenty-four-year-old Aaron Cohn was voted its president, and an eighteen-year-old girl he barely knew was elected treasurer. The only problem with this fact was that the treasurer, Janet Ann Lilienthal, was terrible at arithmetic. Whenever the books had to be balanced, Aaron went to her house to help her. One weekend, Aaron asked Janet Ann and her best friend, Jack Schiffman, to come out to his family farm to ride horses. Janet Ann went; Jack didn't. Aaron and Janet Ann had a lot of fun together. They became close friends and, over time, fell in love.

As the pair saw more and more of each other, Janet's parents cast a wary eye at their daughter's suitor. Although Aaron had joined the temple when he returned from the university and had a grandfather who was born in Germany (before moving to Russia), the Lilienthals still believed that Germanic roots were superior to those of Eastern Europe. Even though they admired Aaron, they weren't sure that his and Janet Ann's differences could be overcome. Undaunted, Janet Ann kept bringing Aaron home, and with time her parents came to appreciate what Aaron was made of.

The Lilienthals' deep family roots extended back in Southern history past the Civil War. Janet Ann's father, Leslie

Ruth Lilienthal adored her only daughter, Janet Ann.

Leslie Lilienthal Sr. owned the fashionable ladies clothing store, Kayser-Lilienthal, in downtown Columbus.

Lilienthal, had grown up in Selma, Alabama. He met his future wife when a high school basketball injury led to blood poisoning in his elbow, and Leslie's family rushed him to Johns Hopkins for treatment. The doctors removed his elbow, and while he was recuperating in the Baltimore hospital, Ruth Gump, a local girl, came to visit him. Ruth was a "modern woman." Leslie had never seen anything like her and fell head over heels in love.

When they married in 1919, Leslie was working in a Selma clothing store owned by the Kayser family. He had a talent for buying and selling women's garments. Ruth gave birth to a daughter, Janet Ann, in 1921. Although Ruth loved her new role as mother, she found Selma to be too provincial for her taste. Being a liberated woman, Ruth smoked cigarettes in public, and she dressed in the modern garb of a flapper. It seemed that wherever Ruth went, eyebrows raised, and Ruth felt like a fish out of water.

Her chance to find a more convivial atmosphere came when the Kaysers made Leslie a partner in a new store to be opened in

Janet Ann Lilienthal doted on her younger brother, Leslie.

Columbus in 1923. At the Kayser-Lilienthal Store on Broad Street, Leslie earned a reputation for selling the highest quality clothes, which he ordered in New York several times a year. In the 1930s as Fort Benning began to buzz with incoming military brass, Leslie's customers included the wives of generals George Marshall, George Patton, and "Vinegar Joe" Stillwell. In fact, Leslie Lilienthal was so trusted for his taste and service that when General Patton's daughter, Ruth Ellen Totten, moved to Turkey with her husband on military assignment, she wrote Leslie a note that said only this: "Dear Leslie, I'm in Turkey. I need clothes. Please help." Leslie happily bundled a collection of clothes and packed them off to Turkey.

As successful as he was, Leslie nevertheless encountered a glass ceiling as he rose in Columbus society. In 1923 Leslie looked forward to joining the new country club. Since he had been a member of the country club in Selma, it never occurred to him that he might be excluded. But when he made inquiries his banker informed him that the club was not taking any new members. Leslie deduced they were not accepting Jews as members. The tables were turned a few years later, however, when the Great Depression hit. The club decided to allow six Jewish families to join. Leslie told them, "No thanks." Instead, he helped to build the Officers Club at Fort Benning where he became a charter member.

Leslie's wealth and polish set him apart from Sam Cohn, the profane but honest livery stable owner who wore a diamond horseshoe pin in his lapel and bought corporate stocks with the zeal of a professional gambler. Sam enjoyed attending the livestock auctions on weekends in Atlanta. He and other cattlemen stayed at the gracious Robert Fulton Hotel, and on Saturday nights, Sam could usually be found holding court at the Ship Ahoy Lounge across the street. Aaron loved to drive over from Athens with his friends. Sam bought them all drinks and entertained them with hilarious stories.

Sam loved to take a drink, and when his doctor told him drinking was bad for his heart condition, the news devastated Sam. When that doctor retired, Sam went in for his checkup with the young doctor who replaced him, Dr. Clarence Butler, and asked him if he could have an occasional drink.

"Sure you can," said the physician.

Sam crowed that he had found the smartest doctor around. "He's a *real* doctor," he told everyone.

Whenever Sam went out of town, Etta packed his bag for him. Sam was fastidious about his appearance. He wore monogrammed lavender silk shirts and tailor-made suits. In his little black traveling case, he carried a change of clothes, baking soda for the indigestion that constantly plagued him, and a bottle of White Horse scotch.

One weekend, he traveled to Montgomery to a family Bar Mitzvah. The caterer, who came from Birmingham, had an identical black case. When Sam left the party to catch the train for home, he picked up the wrong case but didn't realize his error until he had traveled many miles from Montgomery. When he opened the case to retrieve his scotch, he discovered the valise contained nothing but aprons. In a rage, he threw the contents out the train window.

Meanwhile back in Birmingham, the caterer opened her black case only to find Sam's things. She deduced from the monogram on his shirt that the case belonged to Sam and returned his case with a note asking him to please return hers. Sam sent her a check for her losses. His family told and retold this story, and Sam took the ribbing good-naturedly.

Even though Aaron and Janet Ann came from different

backgrounds, they continued to enjoy each other's company, and they grew closer as the weeks rolled by. Both of them were great dancers, and they both enjoyed watching sports. Aaron could not imagine sharing time with a woman who did not like sports. In 1940 when he won the region's most prestigious tennis contest, the Chattahoochee Valley Tennis Tournament, Janet Ann was there to cheer him to victory.

Aaron trains at Chicamauga Park near Fort Oglethorpe in 1939.

CHAPTER 5

DUTY CALLS

Offsetting Aaron's blossoming romance and his rising tennis accomplishments was the depressing international news. A brewing world war threatened to call Aaron away from Columbus a second time. He devoured newspaper reports on the growth of the German Nazi Party. Understanding fully the danger it posed to Jews and other minorities, Aaron saw its leader, Adolph Hitler, as a demon bent on world domination.

In September 1939 France and England finally declared war on Germany after the Nazi government invaded Poland and Czechoslovakia. In the spring of 1940 Hitler began his invasion of Holland, Belgium, and Luxembourg then moved on France. After all that his family had sacrificed because of anti-Semitism, when Aaron read of these events he wanted to shoot Adolph Hitler himself.

When the Nazis captured Paris in June 1940, Aaron could take it no longer. He told George Palmer that with Hitler turned loose on the world he couldn't practice law any more. He wrote a letter to the Department of the Army, telling them he wanted to be placed on active duty. A full week passed before he told Janet Ann he was leaving.

Palmer offered to contact his friends in Washington to get Aaron a good assignment, and Aaron briefly considered joining the JAG Corps, but he really wanted to serve with the troops.

With his life-long experience with horses, nothing but the cavalry would do. Ironically, as he committed to being a horse-riding warrior, the army was abandoning its commitment to the horse. The Second World War would be the first fully mechanized war, and Aaron would soon be riding through Europe on an armored half-track instead of a galloping steed.

In November 1940 Lieutenant Cohn received orders to report to the 4th Infantry Division. He had imagined any number of posts to which he might be assigned—the Presidio, the Philippines or down along the Texas border where most of the horse cavalry units met. So he was surprised and a bit embarrassed to learn that his first post was only eight miles away, where the newly organized 4th Motorized Infantry Division awaited his service in the reconnaissance troop. The paymaster at Harmony Church, Fort Benning, told him as he issued him sixty-four cents, "I don't know what sort of a soldier you will make, but you at least have the distinction of receiving the smallest travel pay I've ever allotted."

Aaron was disgruntled to see on his "66-1" form that someone had typed "Hebrew" beside his nationality.

"I'm an American!" he protested, but he was told, "This is the way the army does it."

In his first months of active duty Aaron was a cavalryman without a cavalry unit. The army designated him as an assistant provost marshal with the military police of the 4th Infantry Division. While Aaron was happy to be actively serving his country, some of the inevitable adjustments to military life came hard. Aaron walked out of the mess hall one day, eating an apple, when he encountered the division's inspector general. Only after Aaron saluted did he realize he still had the apple in his right hand.

Commanding Officer Bill Quinn informed Aaron he had made a bad impression. "Go mend it," he ordered.

When Aaron went to speak to the inspector general, he said, "I'm sorry. I didn't mean to show disrespect. I regret my actions."

Lt. Aaron Cohn's first military post was at nearby Fort Benning with the 4th Infantry Division.

Treating him as though he were an amateur, the officer lectured Aaron on the superiority of the "regular army" versus the "citizen army." As far as he was concerned, Aaron's mistake was an example of why an army of volunteers would never prevail. Aaron held his peace, but in the years to come he would often think of this man and how wrong he proved to be.

Although Aaron was able to live at home during his time with the 4th Infantry Division at Fort Benning, even his family home was beginning to resemble an army post. Next door to the Cohn home, the Ninth Street USO opened in 1941. The National Catholic Community Service Agency and the Jewish Welfare Board, both of which had offices in this building across from the courthouse, sponsored this second USO location to open downtown. Etta Cohn's living room became an adjunct to the new soldier center on Ninth Street, providing a home atmosphere to homesick northern boys. Adding to the number of soldiers whom Etta now cooked for were Aaron's new acquaintances from Fort Benning.

Living at home had its drawbacks, however. One stormy, autumn day Aaron suffered with the flu, and his mother sent him up to his room to rest. But Aaron was the post's officer of the day and unbeknownst to him was needed to conduct an inquest. When the call rang in to order him to report for duty, his mother answered it before Aaron could reach the downstairs phone. He heard Etta tell the caller that her son could not possibly report for duty.

"You want him to come out to the base *now*? Oh no. That's not possible. Lieutenant Cohn doesn't feel well, and it's raining," she said.

Aaron pleaded with his mother, "Mama, give me the phone. You'll get me court-martialed!"

But Etta continued. "What kind of an army is this that would send a boy out on a day like this?"

Lieutenant Cohn was still posted at Fort Benning when he asked Janet Ann to marry him. Everyone had thought their romance wouldn't last, and the Lilienthals were as skeptical as any. Aaron was almost six years older than Janet Ann. They came from two different social circles. Besides, there was a war going on, and that meant that Janet Ann would surely have to leave her family to follow her soldier-husband. Aaron was not offended that Janet's parents doubted the success of their union. After all, Janet Ann was their only daughter, and he thought they *should* be protective of her. Leslie Lilienthal offered a compromise.

"Why don't you just wait until the war is over?"

Aaron took this proposal under advisement and bided his time. His patience eventually paid off. One day Leslie capitulated. He told his daughter, "Let's go down to the store and pick out your trousseau."

They married at the beautiful antebellum home that had been converted into the Harmony Club on June 19, 1941. The fact that they did not stand under a chuppah, or canopy, during the ceremony shocked some of Aaron's kinsmen. A few of them complained to Etta, but she would have none of it. She told them how proud she was to have Janet Ann and the Lilienthals as family, and since they were hosting the wedding, "whatever they do is all right with us."

For their honeymoon Aaron and Janet Ann thought of going to Florida, but the Lilienthals insisted they go to New York instead. With a polio epidemic active at the time, Janet Ann's parents thought going north would be safer. Again, Aaron conceded. They stayed at the Astor, and on the way home stopped in Baltimore so Janet Ann could visit her grandmother.

"How many grooms agree to visit their wife's grandmother on their honeymoon?" Aaron teased, but really, he didn't mind.

When they returned to set up housekeeping, Janet Ann realized she did not know the first thing about cooking or cleaning. A neighbor had to show her how to open a can, and her first meal was a disaster. Aaron bit into a piece of fried chicken only to find it so raw that blood ran out of it.

He said, "That's okay, honey. I'll just eat the green beans." He took one bite and spit them out. Janet Ann had misread the directions on the package of frozen beans and had seasoned them with a half-cup of salt. Janet Ann burst into tears, but Aaron hardly noticed the miserable meal. His mind was on the war.

Organization of the army was fluid at that stage. On 8 December 1941 the US officially entered the war on the day following the bombing of Pearl Harbor. On that day, the Chief of Cavalry ordered all cavalry officers to return to cavalry units. Aaron reported to the 4th Reconnaissance Troop of the 4th Infantry Division (soon to be designated the 4th Reconnaissance Battalion). Leaving the work of assistant provost marshal, Lieutenant Cohn was overjoyed to be joining this highly mobile cavalry unit as a cavalry officer.

About a week after Pearl Harbor the 4th Infantry Division moved its home to Camp Gordon. Janet Ann accompanied Aaron to Augusta, and they rented a room in the basement of the Bon Air Hotel. She used Sterno to heat soup and learned by trial and error the rudiments of keeping house. Balancing their checkbook was beyond her mathematics acumen, and one day the division headquarters called Aaron to inform him they were overdrawn. Embarrassed, he asked Janet Ann how this could have happened. She protested that they could not possibly be overdrawn. There were still *lots* of checks in their checkbook.

Occasionally Leslie Lilienthal secretly mailed Janet Ann money. Aaron would have been too proud to take it. Janet Ann didn't *look* like she was in need of money. Her wardrobe still came from the exclusive Kayser-Lilienthal store. Her clothes were so beautiful, in fact, that they caused some army wives to resent her for dressing better than the battalion commander's wife. For this and other reasons, Janet Ann never found life as an army wife to be a match for her, but she loved her husband, and there was a war going on. She would do the best she could.

When the army realized Aaron was an attorney, they began borrowing him away from his other duties to work on court-martials. He defended a Puerto Rican soldier from New Jersey who got into trouble for causing a ruckus after he was not allowed to sit in either the "white" section of the Augusta movie theater

or the "black" section of another establishment. On his behalf, Aaron explained to the court how impossible it was for a man of mixed race to live in the segregated South, and he suggested the man be returned to Fort Dix rather than be punished further. The authorities agreed, and noting Aaron's excellent skills as an attorney, they began assigning him as a prosecutor.

While prosecuting was an easier job than defense, Aaron found that spending so much time with court-martials

Not long after their marriage in 1941, Janet Ann Cohn was voted one of the best dressed women in Columbus.

to the neglect of his other work made it difficult for him to get promoted. Acting as a lawyer in a combat branch caused him to be passed over several times. Even so, he had no intention of going into the JAG Corps. He was born to ride in the cavalry.

It was at about this time that Aaron received a distressing call from his father. After Sam Cohn's horse and mule sales had declined because of farm mechanization, Sam had closed his livery stable downtown and bought land on Schatulga Road where he specialized in cattle sales. Distinguished gentlemen farmers like W. C. Bradley, Curtis Jordan, and Tom Buck wouldn't dream of buying their cattle, mules, or horses from anyone else. But just as things were going well for him, Sam had some bad news to report.

"Son, the government is taking my land," he told Aaron by telephone.

To enlarge Fort Benning, the government was claiming land adjoining the post under the right of eminent domain. The government offered Sam a pittance of its value, and he was heartsick over losing his property without just compensation when he needed so badly the pastureland for his large herd of cattle.

"Papa, you know you can fight them on this," said Aaron.

"What? I can't believe you'd even suggest that! I would *never* fight the United States!"

Sam's loyalty to the United States cost him six hundred acres of his eight-hundred-acre farm, and the hardest part to accept was that the army never used this land. At the end of the war the government deeded the idle parcel to Muscogee County. Sam had lost a sizable portion of his farm for no great purpose.

Late in 1943 as the cavalry formally acknowledged the end of the era of the horse, the old 3d Horse Cavalry transformed into the three tank battalions of the 10th Armored Division. A new "3d Cavalry Group, Mechanized," consisting of two squadrons of about 750 men each (the 3d and the 43rd), inherited the old Indian-fighting regiment's name and its colors.

Members of the new cadre of the 3d Cavalry convened to organize themselves at Fort Riley, Kansas. The plan was for it to remain separate from any division, answering directly to the corps commander. Its primary mission was battle reconnaissance. Like scouts, the 3d Cavalry, also known as the "Brave Rifles," was to be the eyes and ears of XX Corps (or any other division to which they might temporarily be attached). In battle they would be responsible for patrolling the flanks and occasionally securing the high ground in advance of the infantry. Additionally, the corps commander expected them to collect valuable information by which he could make intelligent decisions in combat.

This 1,553-man unit commanded by Col. Frederick W. Drury represented a conglomerate of experiences. Some of the officers graduated from West Point; some, like Aaron, were university ROTC graduates. The "non-com" contingent came from the 4th Horse Cavalry of Fort Meade, South Dakota, and the remainder was made up of green draftees from upstate New York and the Chicago area.

These draftees were a mix of farm boys, factory workers, and students—a large number of whom were first-generation Americans from Italian, Polish, and other Eastern European descent. Aaron shared a common heritage with these young men who averaged less than twenty years old. Like him, they saw Germany as their natural enemy. As the war progressed he came to admire their tough resourcefulness more and more.

In the organization of the new cavalry unit, Aaron became a captain. The new cadre was dispatched to Camp Gordon, so Aaron returned to Augusta for his second term and focused on transforming draftees who hardly knew their left foot from their right into battle-ready soldiers. The training at Camp Gordon was described as "rigorous and constant. Each man had to be able to operate every vehicle and shoot every weapon in the Group."[1]

Also in Aaron's company were some hard-nosed veteran non-coms who naturally resented a newcomer like Captain Cohn. To break the ice, Aaron called a meeting. He passed around a box of cigars and told them to light up. Then he asked them to introduce themselves. After they took turns relating such personal information as their number of years' experience, Aaron finally spoke.

"I know what you're thinking. I have been on active duty in the army for only three years, so how am I going to lead you guys? But let me tell you something. I care about you. You are my family. If you need me for anything, I'll be there for you."

Sergeant Schmidt stood and congratulated Aaron on making "a great, damn speech." He said, "I don't know how long you'll be in the army, but that will probably rank as the best speech of your life."

Although he could be tough when necessary, Aaron quickly earned a reputation as a caring leader. He remembered not only his men's names but their home towns too. He wanted them to know he did not consider them merely cannon fodder, but flesh and blood compatriots. Because of this attitude, it seemed everywhere Aaron went, recruits walked up to him and said, "Sir, I've got a problem."

Sergeant Shanks, a very efficient, red-headed mess officer with twinkling blue eyes was one of the subordinates who asked Captain Cohn for his help. Shanks was responsible for feeding the men, and he had two guys—Jewish soldiers from New York— who refused to eat. For the two weeks they had been there, they had reported to the mess hall, looked at their food, and turned it down. Shanks was afraid they would starve. Aaron told the sergeant to send the pair to him.

They walked in slouching, displaying no respect for Cohn's rank or for the army in general. Aaron ignored the affront because he could see immediately what the problem was. He told them he understood that they came from religious homes.

"What business is it of yours?" they sneered.

"Listen," Aaron said. "If you think I'm going to run a kitchen according to Jewish dietary laws, you're crazy. But are you aware that in times of war, you are excused from practicing kosher?"

The boys' eyes widened. "Really?" they said.

Aaron showed them the book of edicts from the Rabbinical Conference, which had always held that soldiers were free of dietary laws. The young men broke out in grins. Two weeks later, Sergeant Shanks said to Aaron, "How did you do it? Anyone can teach a man how to fire a weapon or operate a tank, but how did you get these men to *eat*?"

Aaron laughed and said this would remain one of the great

secrets of World War II. But from that day on, Shanks was heard to say many times, "I've got the smartest CO in the army! Why he can convince a man to eat when he doesn't even want to."

Col. Fred Drury also saw potential in Captain Cohn. The 3d Cavalry's commanding officer was delighted to learn of Cohn's stellar college tennis career because Drury loved to play and was in need of a doubles partner. Even with the added pressure of playing with the cavalry commander, Aaron relished this last opportunity to play before he packed off to war.

Observing Aaron both on and off the court convinced Drury that Cohn would make a great staff officer. He sent Aaron to Command General Staff School at Fort Leavenworth, Kansas, for training as a regimental staff officer. As a mere captain Aaron sat shoulder to shoulder with majors and colonels. The curriculum of this, the fourteenth wartime class at Leavenworth, had been condensed from nine months to ninety days because of the exigencies of war. But again Aaron's ability to remember information easily afforded him some spare time. Aaron never left the campus during his stay at Fort Leavenworth. He played tennis every afternoon with some British officers.

As absorbed in military life as he was, Aaron's heart still lay in Augusta at this time. Janet Ann was pregnant and due to give birth any day. Finally, on 9 August 1943, Aaron got the long-anticipated phone call. A baby girl named Gail had made him a father. A faculty member, noting Aaron's elation, told him to take the rest of the day off.

"You won't be any good today anyway," he told him.

In September 1943, Aaron returned to the Augusta garage apartment on Walton Way behind Dr. Robert Greenblatt's home where Janet Ann waited to introduce him to his baby girl. Holding this precious child, Aaron knew he would never be the same.

He had returned from Kansas as the 3d Squadron's S-3 officer. His new duties required that he lead the planning and operations effort of one of the two squadrons of the 3d Cavalry. Aaron divided his time between his family and his work, and his life filled to the brim with both challenges and satisfaction.

In early 1944 he received a promotion to the rank of major and became the S-3 officer of the entire 3d Cavalry. Aaron was now working intimately with Colonel Drury in their final preparations for Europe and overseeing the training of many, including draftees from the Ivy League schools, who disliked being trained by volunteers from southern states like Tennessee and South Carolina and Georgia—young men of little formal education and hard-to-understand accents but who were great troopers.

"I'm so much better educated than they are," the Ivy Leaguers complained.

Aaron told them in no uncertain terms: "Listen to me good. We are training men to be killers. We are not going to defeat Hitler according to who uses the best English. Your mama will one day be glad that you had these guys as officers because they are going to save your life. They'll take you out on a patrol and teach you how to knock a squirrel out of tree at four hundred yards. And they'll bring your mama's boy back home."

Finally, after months of intense training at Gordon and also in maneuvers in Tennessee, it was time for the 3d Cavalry to

join the war. In the spring of 1944 Camp Gordon ordered all personnel to send their dependents home immediately before the group itself left for combat. On a corner near the Camp Gordon parade ground Aaron hugged his baby girl tightly, kissed

Troop Commander Aaron Cohn stands in regimental formation with the 3d Cavalry at Camp Gordon.

Janet Ann, and then waved as they rode away in the family car. A hired driver drove Aaron's girls home to Columbus to live with his in-laws. He mentally preserved this final glimpse of his daughter like a snapshot he would take with him to war. Little Gail was sitting up front and center in her infant seat, turning a toy steering wheel left and right, as though she were in charge of where she was going.

Cohn assists Col. Frederick W. Drury (left) during maneuvers in Louisiana.

Aaron would not see his family again until the war ended, and no one could predict how long that would take. What lay ahead was shrouded in mystery, but even with the best of outcomes all of the Cohns would be changed forever by the war. In a few months, Janet Ann would receive devastating news from the War Department, but it would not relate to Aaron.

A few days after all the dependents left Augusta, the men of the 3d Cavalry boarded a troop train that chugged up the Eastern Seaboard to Boston, Massachusetts. At the bustling US Army pier awaited the *HMS Aquitania,* the world's fourth largest passenger ship now stripped of its finery and converted for war. Aaron, who ranked as the acting executive officer for the ocean crossing, was among the first to locate his bunk near the gangplank. Standing on the upper deck, he watched as an endless line of duffel bag-laden soldiers snaked down the pier and into the bowels of the ship.

A captain, who also hailed from the South but whom Aaron

did not know, detected Cohn's southern accent and came over to stand with him at the railing as they watched a number of dark-haired, darker-skinned medical officers file past them.

The captain said to Aaron, "It looks like we're gonna have a bunch of Jews on this ship."

Aaron eyed the captain and said, "Well, if they're Americans, I'll be proud to fight with them by my side."

The captain turned to Aaron and said, "Let me tell you something about Jews. They never go into combat if they can help it. They never volunteer. They are always looking for a cushy job. They're just not good soldiers."

Aaron held out his hand to the captain. "Let me introduce myself. I'm Maj. Aaron *Cohn*." The man's eyes widened as he

Aaron taught civilians interested in entering the reserves at the CMTC (Citizens Military Training Corps) camp at Fort Oglethorpe.

realized his comments to this major were said with prejudice.

Then Aaron let him know how he felt about it: "And where were you in 1940 when I volunteered for a combat branch—the cavalry? Everything you've said is a bunch of crap. You ought to be fighting with the Nazis!"

Thoroughly disgusted, Aaron turned and walked away. Here he was, on his way to slay the biggest Jew-hater of all, and he would be relying on men like the captain to watch his back. Little did Aaron know how deeply his words touched the captain. Later in Europe, the man looked up Aaron more than once to apologize.

"I didn't know what I was talking about," he told him. "I learned all that from my family."

But on this night in Boston, their last night of revelry before going to a war that would surely claim a number of them, the city welcomed the cavalry officers dressed in their breeches and boots. Aaron made instant friends with recent graduates of OCS, VMI, UGA, Norwich, Arizona, Culver, New Mexico Military Institute, and Texas A&M. They were young, and they were smart. The average age of the officers was between twenty-two and thirty, and the enlisted men averaged only nineteen years old.

Before the night was over, the guys had downed more than a few drinks, ending up at Copley Plaza, where, to the horse soldiers' delight, a carousel operated in the hotel lobby. Around and around they rode on the last horse they were liable to mount during the war.

CHAPTER 6

OVER THERE

The morning after Aaron and his buddies painted the town in Boston, the unescorted *Aquitania* left the harbor and began zigging and zagging its way across the Atlantic Ocean. By staying on an unpredictable course, they made it difficult for the German submarines to line up their torpedoes to fire on them. The men also took comfort in the fact that, as one of the fastest ships on the ocean, the *Aquitania* could outrun, if necessary, the German U-boats (heavily fortified submarines). The enlisted men slept eight to a stateroom, and those who weren't seasick ate a diet of what Sgt. Edward Migdalski described as "greasy boiled pork, floating among other greasy unmentionables of nondescript color."[2] By then it had become abundantly clear that their "free ocean cruise to Europe" would not get a rating of first class.

En route to Europe, Aaron led safety drills in case torpedoes struck the ship. He quietly noted that there did not seem to be enough life boats to seat every passenger. He also studied maps of France, hoping to memorize the location of every berg so that when they landed he would be well versed in French geography.

Listening to the ship's radio on 22 June, Aaron learned of the commencement of Operation Overlord. The Allies full-scale invasion of the continent had finally begun as two US airborne divisions followed by some 4,000 ships and 600 warships, 10,000 planes, and 176,000 Allied troops landed along a series of beaches between Cherbourg and Le Havre. The world held its breath to see if the Americans could do what the British and the French had been unable to do—turn back the conquering Germans.

After nine days out of the sight of land, the *Aquitania* motored into the Firth of Clyde and slipped into its berth at Port Glasgow, Scotland. As the men of the 3d Cavalry disembarked, a band of bagpipers on the dock welcomed them to the war with mournful drones unlike anything most of the men, including Aaron, had ever heard before.

From there, the cavalry group boarded trains for England's Royal Artillery College on the Salisbury Plains. There they drew their equipment and vehicles and rushed to get all of it in first-class shape for combat before crossing the English Channel.

As they underwent more training, they watched demonstrations of all the German mines they soon would encounter. All agreed the worst was the one called the "Bouncing Betty," made of one hundred steel balls that fired into one's private parts from the ground.

When Aaron and the staff realized they were badly in need of fifty caliber machine guns, they put their best (and most unlikely) scrounger to work on finding some. True to his nature, Chaplain K. K. Cunningham produced just what they needed with little time to spare.

They spent their off-hours huddled around a radio, listening to the reports of the ongoing Normandy landings, but occasionally Aaron walked into Salisbury for sightseeing. One day as he passed an old stone church, Aaron was mortified to see two GIs boozed up and fighting right under the church window during a service. Cohn broke up the fight and apologized to the vicar. Another day as Aaron rode down a Cheltenham street, he spied an old friend from Columbus walking in the rain. Butch Page of the 2nd Armored Division had already seen action in Sicily and would soon join the invasion of Europe.

Aaron yelled at Butch, "Captain, get over here!"

Butch had no idea whom this major was who had singled him out, but he double-timed it over to Aaron's jeep only to discover Aaron's grinning countenance.

"You so and so," Butch smiled.

Just when Aaron could not stand the tension of waiting any longer for action, Colonel Drury ran up to him yelling, "We got a mission! We got a mission! Start working on plans for Brest."

Aaron looked at the map and noted that the French port city lay on a peninsular fortified by at least three elite German divisions. The port was also the base of the "wolf packs" of U-boats, which had been preying on Allied ships.

"Who's going to be with us?" Aaron asked his CO.

Drury didn't know who would be supporting them for this invasion. As the news of their assignment filtered down to others, a number of officers who knew of Aaron's legal background asked him to draw up their wills. Luckily for them, the army's plans for employing the 3d Cavalry Group changed just before they left England.

The group received orders to proceed to Southampton to board an LST (Landing Ship Tank) that would transport them across the English Channel. The two squadrons of the 3d Cavalry split up to land at different points along the Normandy coast. A port battalion was supposed to meet them on the beach to help them unload, but when Aaron's group arrived they were nowhere to be seen, and the merchant marines on board his LST refused to help, saying it "wasn't in their contract."

"Hey, don't we belong to the same country?" said Aaron. "Aren't we all trying to defeat the Nazis? They need us at Mortain."

The man answered with a look that said he would not be budged. Aaron was anxious to get to Mortain, France, where the enemy was counter attacking, and the Allies needed more armor. Just when Aaron was beginning to panic, the port battalion showed up.

At dusk on 8 August 1944, Aaron landed at Utah Beach with the 3d Squadron, commanded by Lt. Col. Marshall Wallach—a magnificent officer, West Point graduate in the Class of 1938, and dear friend of Aaron Cohn. Meanwhile the 43rd Squadron invaded nearby Omaha Beach. When the LSTs rumbled onto the beaches, their bows opened wide to spit out thousands of men riding hundreds of combat vehicles and armed with tons of war materiel.

The 3d Cavalry's squadrons drove onto the beaches and kept moving southward as the sun set behind them. They picked their way through a polka dot pattern of bomb craters, most of them measuring six feet deep and fifteen feet across. Here Aaron saw dozens of wrecked gliders that had fallen from the sky during the initial invasion. He also ran into his old wrestling coach from the 1935 Columbus YMCA team, Col. Fay Smith. This was the man who, while demonstrating a headlock, had given Aaron a cauliflower ear.

For the first several miles, military police were posted at every road junction to point in the direction they were to go. After penetrating several miles into the French countryside, they bivouacked for the night. For once no one had to tell the men to clean their weapons. Everyone's mind was on his first encounter with the enemy. Incredulously, Aaron conceded when his loyal mess sergeant, Sergeant Shanks, insisted he give Cohn a hair cut then and there. And if he were not already caught off guard by sitting still for a hair cut at such a tense moment, when Aaron looked at Shanks's handiwork he was thoroughly surprised. He had been shaved bald.

At this same assembly point the 3d Cavalry learned that they were being assigned to Lt. Gen. George S. Patton's Third Army. That night few slept as they lay on the open ground. The next morning Maj. Gen. Walton Walker of XX Corps gave Colonel Drury the 3d Cavalry's first combat mission. The Americans had discovered a crease in the German lines just below Le Mans. They would head right toward it.

The 3d Cavalry was to move out smartly to catch up with and then pass through the swiftly moving Third Army. At that point, the "3d Cav" would become the spearhead of the XX Corps's advance into Germany. The cavalry was ordered to move south through the town of Avranches then head east and southeast, and as they went, the two squadrons were to spread out to cover an eighty-mile-wide swath. As they proceeded, they were to inspect every road, reporting on enemy location and strength, artillery positions, and mine fields. Walker told Drury to expect a German counterattack near Mortain, lying due east of Avranches.

This patch or insignia identifies the 3d Cavalry Group, "the eyes and ears of XX Corps" during World War II.

On the morning of 10 August they moved out. Aaron rode in the mobile command post from which all orders originated—a half-track with mounted fifty caliber machine guns and a gun crew. He scanned the passing countryside in wonder. Here and there the remnant of a wall indicated where a house or barn had stood. Near the coast, the branches of the scraggly trees were still caked with the dust of the battles of D-Day. The city of Avranches was particularly battered, the roofs of all its buildings splayed open to the sky.

The 3d Cavalry then turned southeast and passed through or near the towns of Vitre, Laval, Angers, La Fleche, and Le Mans and began to encounter pockets of resistance from German infantry and tanks. The more the towns lay in rubble, the more jubilant the inhabitants were. Cries of "Vivent les Americains!" and "Merci! Merci!" made the men feel a bit embarrassed, for they had not yet earned the accolades.

Cohn received a radio inquiry from one of his men near Orleans. "Major Cohn, two beautiful women just jumped in my vehicle. What do I do?" he asked.

"Get rid of 'em, damn quick!" replied Cohn. Other men of the "3d Cav" received bottles of champagne and other presents, which were thrust at them as they rumbled by.

Motoring down the dusty French roads of late summer, they realized quickly that what they had learned at their tactical school at Camp Gordon did, in fact, work. If they flanked the Germans, the enemy usually fled in fear of being cut off and surrounded. Nevertheless, there was plenty of fighting to be done, mostly on the roads and in the villages. Along the way, they passed the bodies of dead German soldiers scattered in the ditches. They saw columns of destroyed German vehicles and burned out tanks, some lines of them extending as long as ten miles. Most of this destruction had been the work of the American P-47 fighter aircraft that preceded them.

They were moving so swiftly now that they were surprising both the German and the American high commands. At Angers they found several warehouses loaded with the best of French whiskey, which the Germans had not had time to take with them when they were routed. Obviously, the Germans had expected to stay for a long time, but now they were on the run.

Situated on the right flank of the invading American troops, the 3d Cavalry rolled up the Loire River Valley. The bulk of the German force lay south of them in anticipation of an attack by the Allies from the Mediterranean. (This came later with the entry of the Seventh Army.) With no friendly forces lying to their south, the 3d Cavalry was extremely vulnerable, a fact Aaron was particularly aware of as he executed orders for each day's operations. But luck was on their side.

At Blois, the cavalry turned northeast and passed through Chateaudun, Orleans, Rambouillet, and Chartres. Some members of the Third Cav met Ernest Hemingway, who was staying in a private home with a bunch of Frenchmen near Rambouillet. At Chartres, XX Corps command reported that the Americans already held the city, but a high-ranking American officer who was standing atop his tank there was killed. Everywhere they went, the situation was so fluid, they never knew what to expect. The armor cleared the roads by sweeping back the Germans, but after they had passed, the Germans sometimes returned to ambush the next troops.

The confusion and the swiftness by which they were moving caused the two squadrons of the 3d Cavalry to get separated. For a time, the regimental staff didn't know where the 3d Squadron was. Executive Officer Phil Davidson sent Aaron out in a jeep with a driver to find them. Armed with little more than a map, Major Cohn searched the countryside for the missing squadron, driving up to XII Corps headquarters and to other units to ask if they had seen them in the midst of a fluid and dangerous front. Either the Germans or the Americans easily could have killed Aaron at this time, but somehow he found the 3d Squadron and showed them how and where to rejoin the 43rd.

By the last week of August they were fighting their way through the Forest of Fontainebleau toward the Seine River. They already had earned a reputation for their swift, surprising moves. Others began to call them the "Ghost Troops." They ran through the German lines like a good football halfback. No one could predict just where or when they would break through because they were moving so much faster than the enemy could anticipate. The cavalry was so far ahead of the bulk of the American force that they often surprised German soldiers in the middle of a meal, completely unaware that the cavalry was anywhere near them.

The 3d Cavalry was only thirty miles south of Paris when they crossed the Seine at Melun and Fontainebleau. They had orders not to go into Paris because the 1st French Armored Division, which had been fighting in North Africa under Le Clerc, was given the honor of liberating Paris.

The 3d Cavalry's ultimate destination was Berlin, so they continued east, setting their immediate sights on seizing the bridge at Verdun, the French city straddling the Meuse River, which flowed through a bright green valley in the Argonne Forest.

During the month of August, the 3d Cavalry had executed a perfect cavalry mission over generally flat terrain. An old, veteran general of World War I told Aaron with unbridled disgust, "You see those woods there?" Pointing to the Argonne Forest on the map, he said, "I spent ninety days there in the last war, and you went through there in two hours!"

On 31 August 1944 they reached Verdun. The Germans

retreated as they arrived, so they took possession of the city with hardly a casualty. Aaron's colleague, Tech. Sgt. Joe Radanovich of the Headquarters Troop of the 3d Squadron passed through Verdun on 1 September and noted in his diary the scenes there.

> There in Verdun, as in all the other liberated French towns and small villages, happiness was on the faces of all the people. Going across the one remaining bridge in the city, over the Meuse, we came soon into the heart of Verdun—past the Citadel, down the main street, through the congested business district. Portions of it were as modern as shops at home. The sidewalks were lined with people; old, young, some laughing, some weeping, mostly old women and men. Here too, as in the other larger towns, I saw the FFI ["French Forces of the Interior"] marching women collaborators down the streets, most of them very young and pretty. But in a short while I knew they would be horrid to look at with their hair sheared off completely from their heads. I counted three groups of about fifteen women each and knew there would be more counted by our troops . . . We went through town and past the great monuments to the soldiers dead of the last war, past military cemeteries where we saw the crosses 'row on row' . . . The countryside outside Verdun in the last war was badly torn, but this time it wasn't so hard hit. On the road out, toward Etaine, the wreckage was unmistakably the 'last mile' for hundreds of Jerries [Germans] whose bodies were already beginning to give out that awful nauseating stench, rotting in the weather, their tanks and wagons and equipment strewn on both sides of the road. Our air support and the 'Jabos' [American P-47s] did a splendid job of ruining most of that planned withdrawal from the Meuse." [3]

CHAPTER 7

TASK FORCE POLK

In his first month in combat, Aaron had become battle-wise and confident, but his biggest challenges lay ahead. The 3d Cavalry next targeted Metz, which guarded the Moselle River in the Alsace-Lorraine region of France on the border of Germany.

When the cavalry reached Alsace-Lorraine, they immediately noticed a difference in the attitude of the citizenry. In this territory, which had been claimed alternately by Germany and France over the centuries, the inhabitants did not come out to greet them as liberators. No one cheered them on. Their doors remained closed. These people were more pragmatic. They were known to own three flags (American, German, and French), and depending on which army was marching through at the moment, they hoisted the corresponding flag.

The 3d Cavalry charged toward Metz so fast, they "ran off the map." With tactical maps no good to them any more, they used Michelin roadmaps to plot their course forward.

Had they not run out of gas at this point, they probably would have arrived in Metz in only another week. But having outrun their supply lines, American vehicles coasted to a stop, immobilized and vulnerable. If the Germans counter attacked now, they were sitting ducks.

Although the Germans did not go on the offensive, they

did take advantage of the break in action to bolster their defenses along the Moselle. Meanwhile the Air Force came to the cavalry's rescue, landing what appeared to be hundreds of DC-3 planes loaded with thousands of filled gas cans in a farmer's field on the Verdun-Etaine highway. With impressive speed the 3d Cavalry was rumbling again toward the Moselle.

However, they would arrive without their CO. When Commanding Officer Colonel Fred Drury decided to accompany a patrol from the 3d Armored Reconnaissance Squadron as it reconnoitered near Metz, he made a grave error in unnecessary exposure. At Gravellote, Germans fired on Drury's jeep. He and his driver took cover, but the Wehrmacht captured them.

Aaron was working in the regimental command post at Verdun when telephone and radio communiqués from the 3d Squadron began pouring in. At length Aaron pieced together that Drury had been captured. The 3d Squadron's Lt. Col. Marshall Wallach led a patrol to the ambush site, but they found only empty vehicles.

Just when it seemed to Aaron that their luck could not get any worse, in walked a "disheveled, bloody, and upset" officer we'll refer to as Captain Jones who had left group headquarters the day before to visit the command post of the 43rd Squadron at Longuyon.[4] While Jones was en route, the 43rd squadron was ordered to move out without his knowledge. Jones, riding with two sergeants, arrived at Longuyon at about the same time that the Germans captured Drury in another sector (unbeknownst to Jones).

Jones realized something was amiss when he saw no sign of the squadron but found farm vehicles blocking the road. At that moment German soldiers began firing on their command car. Although Jones and the sergeants were able to run to safety, the Germans captured the car. In it were the 3d Cavalry's colors.

Not since the Civil War had a US military force lost its colors, and this fact was doubly hurtful because they had been lost without losing a battle. The battle streamers, which recorded the historic troop's battle record from its inception in 1846 during the Mexican War, were taken along with the green and gold 3d Cavalry flag.

Later, when Jones burst into headquarters, he was unaware the colors had been captured. He blurted out that he was sure to be court-martialed because Colonel Drury's clothes had been stashed in the car that was captured. Major Cohn then told him that Drury wouldn't need his clothes after all because he had just been captured.

"Thank God!" cried Jones, and they all had a good, hard, therapeutic laugh before they got back to work. Through and through it had been a bad day for the regimental staff. Col. Fred Drury would not return to them for the remainder of the war. Aaron and the others worked into the night to cover his loss.

One long week passed at the command post before a replacement for Drury arrived, and Cohn got little rest during that week. The new CO was only a lieutenant colonel, but his meritorious record spoke volumes. Graduating in West Point's Class of 1933, he formerly had been executive officer of the 106th Cavalry. Polk had served under Gen. George Patton, and his father had roomed with Patton at Virginia Military Institute. He would soon fulfill everyone's expectations as the kind of leader they hoped for, and many years later Polk would end his career as a four star general officer with great honors. However, at this moment, James H. Polk had much to prove to his men and to himself as he entered the command post on 12 September 1944.

With prominent, black eyebrows and a boyish face, Jimmy Polk held his tall, thin torso erectly as he strode into the room and straight up to Aaron Cohn.

"Who are you?" he demanded.

Aaron replied, "Sir, I am *your* S-3." Aaron stressed that he belonged to Polk because he feared he would be washed out of the job now that Drury was gone. Being a reservist, he did not automatically command the respect of a regular army officer. Aaron would have to prove to Polk that he belonged at his side.

After Cohn introduced himself, Polk looked Cohn over and then walked away without comment. A few minutes later Polk stepped back in.

"I want to issue a five paragraph order. Can you do it?"

Gen. James Polk inscribed this photo to Aaron, "the best regimental S-3 in World War II."

"Yes sir," replied Aaron. "I'm a Leavenworth graduate. I can do it."

In no time, Aaron wrote up the order and gave it to the colonel to read. The CO offered no feedback except to tell Aaron to print it. Aaron took comfort in the fact that Polk had not made a single change.

Perhaps Polk was hard on Cohn because he was nervous about fulfilling his new assignment. Polk had written his wife on 11 September, as he was en route to his new post, expressing his apprehension about what lay ahead for the 3d Cavalry. "The

Germans apparently intend to make a stand along the Siegfried Line that will make it rougher on the people who have to punch through it."[5]

One of Aaron's responsibilities as S-3 officer was to oversee the *efficiency* of the message center, which ran twenty-four hours a day (although not the message center per se). At two a.m. a message came in from XX Corps headquarters while Aaron was snoring in his sleeping bag. The message said, "Meet Comet 6 at 0600 hours." When the young man operating the message center could not make heads or tails out of it, he woke Cohn. Aaron could not understand it either. Exhausted after being up for the better part of three nights, Aaron told the young soldier to follow up on it, then he rolled over and fell soundly asleep.

The next day Lt. Colonel Polk walked into the command post, fuming and holding the message. "I want to know who is responsible for this," he said. He had missed a six a.m. meeting with the corps commander.[6]

The young message center operator, a graduate of Cornell University, panicked, but Aaron spoke up. "Sir, I accept responsibility for the message center. We had not seen this new code before and it looked garbled to us."

Polk gazed at Cohn with steely eyes. For the next thirty days and nights, the CO would ride him hard. Their interactions remained professional but formal. In this tense environment, Aaron tried to concentrate on fighting the Germans, not his CO, but he knew his job was in jeopardy. A report came in from a troop commander that German patrols were invading US artillery positions at a certain location. Lt. Colonel Polk told Aaron to show him on the map where the troop was, and when he did, they realized they were a half-mile off of their objective. Polk moved the commander off the front lines then and there.

Spearheading and screening XX Corps, advanced elements of the cavalry group already had reached the Moselle River by the time Polk arrived. At the eastern edge of the Argonne Forest, neither the Americans nor the Germans had accurate information as to where the other was lurking, so they continually knocked into each another, day and night. Frequent skirmishes kept all of them on edge.

Camping on a wind-swept hill above the river, Aaron and the others at regimental headquarters ate captured German rations and were happy to have them—some good cheese, some canned green beans, and some fresh coffee. But they were soaked to the bone from the constant rains and irritated at the radio reports, which portrayed their action as a cake walk. The rain was turning rivers the size of American creeks into raging torrents the size of the Mississippi. Some units were fighting all day to progress only a hundred yards, and nowhere did they encounter Germans surrendering.

Breaking through the historic fortresses protecting Metz was the key to successfully crossing the river and entering Germany. Over several centuries many different armies had constructed a double ring of forty-three forts to protect this river crossing, and the Nazi army had strengthened these. They also used to their advantage the topography—a combination of rugged terrain and the raging river. The Americans now faced one of the greatest natural barriers any army would ever confront; yet taking Metz was crucial.

While the Germans were well entrenched in their fortifications, they made frequent forays across the river to ascertain how and where the Americans were planning to hit them. Both armies aggressively patrolled every night, and they exchanged artillery fire continually. Their stalemate continued for weeks. The Brave Rifles, who had been so adept at moving forward at lightning speed, now stood immobile on the west bank of the Moselle.

The reinforced cavalry group held a thin twenty-mile line along the river from Thionville to the northern boundary of XX Corps's zone. Behind the cavalry screen waited the 90th Infantry Division, and behind them the 10th Armored Division sat ready to exploit the bridgehead once it opened. To hold this river line, a battalion of 155 howitzers and another of 105 howitzers, a tank destroyer battalion, and an engineer combat battalion supported the 3d Cavalry. On 20 September, this bolstered force of the 3d Cavalry became officially known as Task Force Polk. The first of many wartime task forces had officially been designated.

For the next six weeks, Task Force Polk stood nose to nose with the Germans from either side of the river. The weather was as much a foe as the Germans, with constant rains causing more casualties to "trench foot" than to bullets. And the more it rained the wider and more turbulent became the river. Nevertheless, the regimental staff utilized the countryside to great advantage and kept the Germans guessing right up to the moment they sprung across the river.

Aaron described how they were able to effect their screen.

The method of this successful defense of a river line as a line of departure of a major attack was simple and effective. There were a number of villages along the river, backed by a series of rolling hills. The buildings in the village, made of solid stone and brick construction, formed the core of resistance. They made excellent OPs [outposts] and weapon positions to cover the flat land adjacent to the river and offered a haven to the troops against the elements. (In this rainy autumn, more men were lost to the elements than to enemy action.) The buildings also provided good protection from the enemy artillery positions and from Forts Koenigsmacher and Illange on the east side of the river.

The vehicles accompanied the troops into the towns and were placed in buildings available for action. This provided highly mobile fire power to sweep the flat land of the river valley and also furnished radio communication with all units in the event that wire failed.

During the day, a system of OPs kept

the river under constant surveillance. Wire lines were run back to mortar positions, assault guns, tank destroyer and artillery positions, so that fire could be massed quickly at any given point. The tank destroyers, artillery and assault guns, and organic cavalry weapons fired during the day at targets of opportunity reported by the OPs, and the enemy was made to realize that his slightest movement brought a veritable deluge of fire. These tactics caused him to be more reluctant to assume an offensive attitude and limited his activities to darkness.

At night, heavily armed listening posts were moved down to the river's edge, patrols were sent across the river periodically, and combat patrols worked between strong points to intercept hostile enemy patrols probing into our area. The constant harassing fires of all the heavy weapons during the night created a considerable show of force, gave the enemy no time to relax, and complicated his supply problems. In an effort to keep the enemy off balance, this fire was changed from day to day, with variations in weapons, locations, and routes."[7]

Polk and his staff caught a break in the tedium of holding the west river bank when they commandeered the Chateau d'Etange near Thionville as their command post. Only a mile behind the thin front lines, the luxury they enjoyed here was unnerving after so much privation. They now had "electricity, hot and cold running water and real beds with sheets on them," wrote Polk, who had a private room with a view of a green slope running down to the river. Cohn slept in a sleeping bag on the floor of a room shared by several other staff officers, but he felt just as lucky as his colonel did, although impatient to get moving again.

Aaron was still on Colonel Polk's bad side, but he was making inroads to his CO's heart. The Colonel was terrible with names, yet Cohn remembered not only a man's name but the number of his unit. Whenever an officer paid them a visit, Aaron whispered this information to Polk, who came off looking sharp, and Cohn was pleased that his CO was coming to rely on him more and more.

Adding to the surreal ambience of the new quarters were the First and Second Battalions of the First Regiment of Paris, who camped like gypsies with their goats, pigs, and women just outside Thionville. Colonel Polk called them privately "a bunch of crazy communists . . . intent on killing Germans . . . [whom] DeGaulle didn't want . . . in Paris so nominated them to come up and join the fight." The Twelfth Army Group had passed them off onto the Third Army, who sent them down to the 3d Cavalry. Being the lowest echelon, the Polk Task Force had nowhere else to send them.

The "French Tactique," as the Frenchmen were known, had no uniforms of their own but usually could be identified by the tubes of Bangalore torpedoes they wore crossed over their chests. After the 3d Cavalry supplied them with captured German equipment, Gen. George Patton drove up through the lines to the 3d Cavalry headquarters and, on the way, was surprised to see a German Volkswagon pass, its riders wearing German pot helmets and gesturing peace signs at him.

"Who the hell was that?" asked Patton.

"Sir, that's Colonel Dax, the CO of the French Tactique."

Patton shook his head in amazement.

As confounding as the Frenchmen were, they had their strong suits. Colonel Polk told his wife they were "well versed in ambushing, guerilla warfare and underground activities, but not at all qualified to do well in a front line position." The Frenchmen were not the most reliable of informants, either.

They tended to exaggerate the size of the foe, but they loved killing Germans. They were always telling Aaron, "I want to blow up ze Boche."

For the most part the French Tactique was ungovernable. When the task force issued them three days' rations, they radioed the next day that they were all too sick to carry out their mission. It seems they had eaten all three days' grub in one sitting.

On another occasion the Parisians requested a meeting with 3d Cavalry headquarters. Their sector of responsibility opposed the most heavily fortified area of the SS troops.

"We have a plan we want to submit to you," they told Col. Phil Davidson, the executive officer (a West Point graduate of the Class of 1938 and later Chief of Staff to General Westmoreland in Vietnam).

"We want you to go into the woods and flush out the Germans."

"And where will you be?" asked Davidson.

"We will be in the foxholes along the perimeter and when the Germans run, we will shoot them down like dogs."

Davidson made a counter proposal. The *Americans* would wait on the perimeter for the French to flush the Germans. Because Davidson did not speak French, these negotiations continued for what seemed like hours and generally added to the regimental staff's headaches in managing a diverse task force. When the Frenchmen were finally relieved from duty on the Moselle, Aaron and his comrades were glad to see them go.

In approaching the Moselle, the two squadrons of the 3d Cavalry became separated from each other by the 5th Infantry Division. The 43rd Squadron fanned out to attempt to cover about sixteen miles of river front. Without sufficient manpower, the lines were porous. In several places the Germans held land on the Americans' side of the river. Patrols from both armies continually ran into the other. The whole situation was nerve wracking, and Cohn's job was more complicated by the fact that his two squadrons were separated with faulty communication between them.

Remarkably, the chateau command post received no incoming German shells. Aaron believed the owner had made an agreement with the German army to allow it to stand unharmed. The estate entertained a constant stream of visitors, including war correspondents, who hoped to find a hot bath and a comfortable bed. Some grew jealous of such accoutrements. One visiting general from XX Corps grew furious when Colonel Polk pushed a button at their dinner table and three lovely French maids brought out hot rolls from the kitchen.

Unlike this artillery commander, the 3d Cavalry's esprit de corps enjoyed the spoils of war. Everyone knew living in a chateau was too good to last. As soon as they crossed the river, they would be living in the mud again, so they intended to enjoy it while they could. They felt no need to suffer like the infantry, and this cavalry policy insured a high morale.

By the end of September per Colonel Polk's orders, Aaron was writing plans of operation for a growing number of battalions gathered on the river bank. Janet Ann's letters from home arrived sporadically, and several of them never reached him at all. One letter worried him. In it, his wife alluded to the death of someone close to them, but did not say specifically who had died. The previous letter, which had explained that her brother Leslie (known in the family as "Sonny") had been killed in action near Fort Kerenreaux, France, never reached Aaron.

Aaron had first met Sonny Lilienthal at the Columbus YMCA. He was a feisty young man who came to idolize Aaron. And when Aaron went off to war, Sonny was not far behind. He graduated from Castle Heights Military Academy then impatiently waited his turn to get into action. Sonny died on 13 September 1944, his third day of combat as an individual rifle replacement, hardly knowing the names of the men on his right or left in F Company of the 175th Regiment, 29th Infantry Division. He had been in the army a total of nine months and was only nineteen years old when he was laid to rest in an American military cemetery in Brittany.

The Star of David marks the tomb of Leslie Lilienthal Jr in the Brittany military cemetery located at St. James, France.

Several more weeks passed before Sonny's death was confirmed to Aaron, and months went by before he had time to grieve for his brother-in-law. In the meantime he worked night and day. During the month of September 1944, Task Force Polk was deployed all the way from Haute Kontz on the north to Uckange on the south. Casualties were generally light except for the Assault Gun Troop of the 43rd Squadron, which had been heavily shelled.

In October artillery and mortar fire continued to pummel

both sides of the Moselle. It seemed that any sort of movement by the Americans during the day drew German fire, and at night the enemy slipped across the river and crept through holes in the thin American lines. By daylight, the Americans usually were able to beat them off, but night after night the Americans never knew where the Germans would attack next.

Part of Aaron's job was to stay in contact with both squadrons of the 3d Cavalry by making visits to their command posts in the early morning whenever ordered to. In such a fluid situation, it was easy to be ambushed. One moment Americans passed down a road, and all was well, but an hour later the Germans waiting in the woods had regrouped and retaken the highway, putting American lives in peril again.

The 3d Cavalry's biggest challenge actually lay with the civilian population in this highly populated industrial area of France where most of the people were pro-German. Civilians cut American communication wires, informed the Germans of their locations, and even sniped at them. When the task force began strictly regulating curfews along the river towns, they were able to control their activities better.

At last the 83rd Infantry Division was ordered to relieve Task Force Polk along the front for a few days' rest. Colonel Polk watched Aaron closely as he planned and directed the relief. All went very smoothly. After weeks of strictly professional dialogue between the two men, Polk finally let down his guard. As they walked out of headquarters together, the Colonel put his arm around Cohn and hugged him tightly.

"Aaron Cohn," he said, "you are mine, and I'll never let you go."

If Polk had asked Aaron to swim the raging Moselle River at that moment, he gladly would have done it. Polk was becoming convinced that Cohn was "the best S-3 in World War II," and Jimmy Polk had become Aaron Cohn's hero for life.

Polk's entire task force finally was finding a place in the commander's seemingly cold heart. The colonel confided in a letter to his wife that his troops had become "real seasoned

troops now and are most condescending to the new arrivals . . .
Our main diversion is telling the new people horror stories about
our close escapes."

In another letter Polk wrote: "The truth of the matter is that
I have a grand bunch of men working for me. We understand
one another, and we like one another, and we are getting the
job done. I'm just about as proud as a man can be about his
outfit; the new 'Brave Rifles' really are good. And a lot of people
besides myself think so."

CHAPTER 8

CROSSING THE MOSELLE

For eight long weeks the 3d Cavalry crouched like a tiger before the Moselle River while corps command strategized how to tear through the Germans' seemingly impenetrable fortifications. Even at night, the cavalry was active, as Aaron later summarized.

> In the defense of the river line involving a large portion of ground, patrolling was aggressive and constant at night. The gaps between the strong points were covered by strong combat patrols on the prowl to prevent infiltrating troops. The men were fully briefed, equipped, well armed and imbued with an aggressive spirit of either 'kill or capture' the enemy.
>
> Patrols sent across the river to capture prisoners, to ascertain the enemy's plans, installations, capabilities, etc., were extremely valuable. Missions were simple, and had limited objectives . . . Armored Vehicles were . . . hidden in the daytime to prevent being a lucrative target, they were brought out at night to form the perimeter defense of the strong

point. Routes were previously reconnoitered so
that when the LP [listening post] reported any
enemy movement, the vehicle rolled to the scene
immediately to destroy the hostile patrol."[8]

In early November, XX Corps made final preparations for
the anticipated assault across the Moselle River. They would cut
off Metz from both the north and the south. Before this push
could begin, however, corps command assigned the 3d Cavalry
the task of capturing the town of Berg and a strategic hill on the
Americans' side of the river (the west).

For weeks the 43rd Squadron had been avoiding this
German-held zone. They believed the cost of taking it was
too high, so they contained it and hoped they could bypass it
altogether. However, it became clear as plans for crossing the
river crystallized that they would need to take the protecting hill,
at minimum, in order to surprise the Germans when they built a
bridgehead near there.

Capturing Hill 226 required two attempts and cost them
several casualties, and, once taken, the corps also ordered
the capture of Berg. So on 5 November an even harder fight
commenced, much of it hand-to-hand. In two hours' time,
American tanks overcame heavy mortar fire and booby traps to
knock out German machine gun outposts. Men on foot and in
jeeps worked in tandem to clear the town house by house.

According to the 3d Cavalry's official history during the two-
hour attack on the city of Berg, they took twenty-four German
prisoners and killed eight. Americans lost four killed and fifteen
injured, mostly from booby traps and mortar shrapnel. As the
Germans retreated, they ran down to the river and jumped into
rowboats to make their escape, but American assault guns cut
them down. As the cavalry group's official history sums it, the
Battle of Berg drew to a close as "the unmanned boats drifted
silently down the Moselle River."

Berg was finally in American hands, and at the nearby city
of Bettembourg, Luxembourg (the 3d Cav's last command post

before crossing the Moselle), the mayor was planning a festive party to honor the American conquerors. But the 3d Cavalry had no time to attend the party. A full assault across the river began on 9 November 1944. The 90th Infantry Division, assembled in the woods behind the 3d Cavalry, crossed south of Berg and north of Thionville. Meanwhile the 95th Infantry Division repared to cross the river south of the 90th Infantry Division, and the 5th Division kept pressure on the forts of Metz.

At two a.m. the infantrymen pushed off and began rowing across the mighty Moselle. When they reached halfway, Germans fired parachute flares, lighting up the entire river valley. The enemy rained down their artillery and mortar on the boats. Casualties were heavy, but eventually the infantry reached the eastern bank only to encounter barbed wire, mines, and even more German fire power.

By dawn the attached engineer battalion had begun building a bridge across the river, and soon the 10th Armored Division crossed with orders to turn north and northeast in the direction of Saarburg, the weakest link in the Siegfried Line. As they marched, the sight of the many infantrymen of the 90th Division who had died in crossing the river sickened them. Bodies "stacked like cordwood six feet high" lined the road.

While they waited for the 10th Armored Division to cross the pontoon bridge into Germany, the 3d Cavalry received a much-appreciated break. For the first time in three months, they were pulled off the front line to enjoy a bath, hot food, and a good night's sleep. Unfortunately, this respite only lasted thirty-six hours.

Aaron grew sick at this time. Chills and fever tormented him, but he feared that if he reported sick, he would be sent to a hospital and lose his unit. After all he and his friends had faced together, the specter of losing them now was worse than any illness. Although he barely could stand, he reported to work each day. After the war he caught pneumonia four times and felt this was a direct result of not treating his illness in Europe.

When they finally crossed the river they had been staring at for two, long months, they once again took their place at the front of the lines that were closing in on Nazi Germany. Aaron was relieved to be on the move again because this is what the cavalry did best. With adrenaline pulsing through their veins, the Brave Rifles steeled themselves to endure whatever was necessary to end this war, once and for all.

Once they put the Moselle behind them, their mission became to reconnoiter aggressively between the Moselle and Saar Rivers below the "Switchline," an east-west extension of the north-south oriented Siegfried Line. The main fortifications of the infamous Siegfried Line also awaited them just west of the Saar River. Only after they penetrated these defenses could they feel they truly had Hitler cornered.

The Siegfried Line, the two hundred mile long defense running along the east bank of the Saar River, consisted of a series of concrete pill boxes armed with cannon and machine guns pointed in all directions. This infrastructure was surrounded by "wire and mines and protected by dragon's teeth," which were concrete posts planted into the ground, strong enough to "stop any tank we have,"

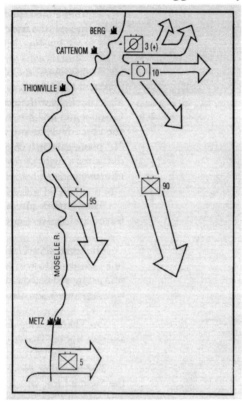

Aaron's map of the attack that drove the Germans out of Metz, France, in November 1944 shows the concerted effort of the 90th Division, the 95th Division, the 5th Division, and the 10th Armored Division. The map accompanied his *Cavalry Journal* article, "A Cavalry Task Force in the Defense of a River Line" in 1945.

according to Colonel Polk.

Behind the dragon's teeth lay an anti-tank ditch, which could measure twenty feet wide by twelve feet deep with two feet of water in the bottom of it. To make planning even more complicated, each of the pill boxes supported each other, so that in firing on one of them, the Americans stood vulnerable to fire from either side as well as from behind them. In some places the

Aaron, second from right, was the Operations and Planning Officer of Task Force Polk.

depth of this defense ran as much as forty to fifty miles. And in one twenty-mile stretch of the line, there were said to be three to four hundred pill boxes.

On 17 November 1944 one unit of the 3d Cavalry crossed the Moselle River into Germany. The regimental staff met on the evening of 18 November to draw plans for the rest of the group's crossing. By the end of the meeting, Cohn and Polk were "exhausted but proud and confident." The Americans had the Germans on the run, and they cheered each other by saying this was surely the beginning of the end. Polk wrote to his wife that night, "Life is busy and exciting . . . Everyone is giving it all that he has got, and we don't intend to stop short of Berlin."

Aaron crossed the Moselle River at a point south of the Switchline and reconnoitered the square of land before him, which was enclosed by the German border to the south, the Siegfried Line to the east, the Switchline to the north, and the Moselle River to the west.

Each night at ten the regimental executive officer, Phil Davidson; Aaron, the Operations and Planning Officer; and Tom Greenfield, who was Aaron's assistant Operations Officer, sat around a table at command post to listen to Polk's plans for the next day's movements. Colonel Polk outlined the broad strokes of how to proceed, then Aaron worked into the night to figure out how to execute the orders, then write instructions as explicitly and briefly as possible, then print and disseminate the order.

Polk thought Aaron "put out the best orders in this Corps." Cohn made it a practice to get Greenfield to read his orders before he printed them. "If you can understand it, they will," he told the ex-collegiate football player.

Polk believed his staff was made of "three fine men that I know and respect and almost love. They would die for me and probably I would die for them. Who knows?"

Every night, they set up a perimeter defense for their most vulnerable hours, and the last thing Aaron did before stretching out in his sleeping bag was to set the "no fire line."

To do this, he passed on the artillery coordinates so they would not kill Americans during the night as they fired over their heads at the Germans. Because his last responsibility before sleeping was so critical to American lives, Aaron usually found it difficult to sleep. Lying in the dark, he mentally went over and over the coordinates, afraid he might have made a miscalculation. But he never made a mistake. No one was lost to friendly fire because of Aaron Cohn.

Sporadically, just before daylight Aaron drove out to locate the units and make sure they were where they reported themselves to be. This was the most dangerous duty he had and led to several close calls. One day he rode down to check on the French Tactique after the unruly, eccentric Frenchmen were causing a hubbub down by the river. When Aaron went out to settle them down, he got caught in a German mortar barrage, begun because the Frenchmen had been needlessly stirring up trouble in the vicinity.

Another close call came the day Cohn walked toward a door that he was unaware had been booby trapped by the 83rd Division, which recently had left the area. Just as Major Cohn reached for the door knob, a trooper grabbed his arm and pulled him backward. If Aaron had opened the door, a grenade wired to detonate would have killed him.

Each day Aaron ran the command office. Staying near the radio at all times when Polk and executive officer Davidson were out, Aaron could communicate and coordinate messages between them and also to and from corps command.

Polk privately referred to Aaron as "the brains" of the three officers while Greenfield, who previously played ball for the Green Bay Packers, he considered to be "the brawn." Polk described Aaron as "a stocky man with red hair, a graduate lawyer from Georgia . . . He has a most unmilitary bearing, but smart as a whip, beautifully educated and a likable personality."

Aaron and Tom Greenfield were an unlikely pair. They reminded Polk of the cartoon strip characters, "Mutt and Jeff," who were also physical opposites. In spite of their stark differences in stature, Aaron and Tom could not have been closer. The giant Greenfield suffered from frequent nightmares. In the darkness, he'd thrash and moan, exclaiming, "They've surrounded us!"

And Aaron would crawl out of his sack to sit on the big man's chest, speaking to him softly to wake and calm him.

Polk privately worried what would befall Aaron if he were captured. The "H" (for Hebrew) on his dog tag gave him away. Being Jewish, Aaron's fate was bound to be horrific because the Germans did not strictly adhere to the rules of the Geneva Convention. So, unlike the average soldier, Aaron was simultaneously fighting a personal and a public war. In both, he had much to gain and much to lose.

In the Saar-Moselle Triangle it seemed that in every village, a fight awaited them. The colonel described their casualties as "not excessive" and kept moving forward. Slowly but steadily they drove back the Germans. Fearing a counteroffensive by the 11th Panzer Division, they welcomed to their task force the 705th Tank Destroyer Battalion, a "self-propelled battalion with high-velocity 76mm guns." Aaron was glad to have them because they were the only Allied outfit on a par with the dreaded Panzers.

CHAPTER 9

UP AGAINST THE SWITCHLINE

The command post was in Perl, Germany, when Jimmy Polk received orders promoting him to full colonel on 21 November 1944. A couple of days later without warning the 3d Cavalry ran into the Switchline and took heavy casualties. At Borg, they received heavy mortar fire and lost some more men. It took a few days before they figured out how to attack this heavily fortified line. To their advantage they now had all the food, men, gasoline, and equipment they needed to get the job done.

The weather continued to challenge them with temperatures near freezing and rain almost daily. They fought the mud as much as the Germans, but no one complained. They knew time was on their side. Thanksgiving Day was spent near the Switchline. The Third Army took great pains to provide a good meal for the men on a day when everyone's thoughts were of their loved ones in America. Aaron and the regimental staff washed down their turkey and dressing and raisin bread with captured German wine at the command post in a small village. One staff member played a Christmas song on a piano while, fifty yards down the road, Germans were shelling the hell out of the place. At that moment Aaron and the others really didn't give a damn. They were celebrating a thoroughly American holiday, come what may.

The enlisted men ate in staggered shifts in occupied churches and schoolhouses all along the front lines. Morale was high. The men were proud of their accomplishments and confident the end was near. The next morning, 24 November, all elements of Task Force Polk began hitting the Switchline.

On 26 November the 3d Cavalry took a short break from the front lines for a hot bath, a treat from the Red Cross donut

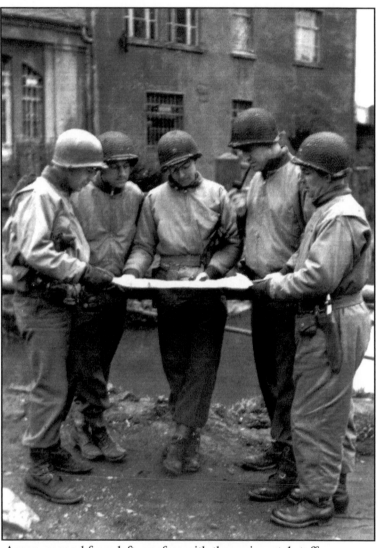

Aaron, second from left, confers with the regimental staff.

truck, and a movie. Their command post was now in a rathskeller just over the border in France. Although it was a relief to be out of the thick of the action, Cohn's duties were as crucial as ever. Colonel Polk and Major Cohn "had a horror of being slipshod when men's lives [were] at stake."

The colonel explained to his wife that war was rarely glamorous. "You should understand that men don't die in the glory of battle in some gallant charge amidst the music of bugles and the roll of drums. They die often in abject fear in dirt, in mud, in filth and exhaustion, and in the taking of some miserable little hill or some dirty little town. There are some glorious moments that transcend all the badness of it, but they are few and far between."

Cohn pored over aerial photographs and studied road and topographical maps before deciding the most efficacious way to reenter the line under the cover of darkness. Two days later on 28 November, the Brave Rifles were back on the frontline with approximately the same artillery, tank destroyers, and engineers attached to them as before. Polk wrote his wife that he had "a harmonious and a smart staff," and he knew that he commanded "a great fighting outfit." Backed up against the Switchline, they relieved the 10th Armored Division and occupied the line from the Moselle River and beyond on their left down to the Saar River on their right where the 10th Armored Division was deployed. Their orders were to keep their side of the Switchline clear of Germans while also scouting likely places to break through it.

The command post that week was "an ordinary size room" filled with six to eight men and "phones, maps, messengers popping in and out." Other men gathered there to receive orders or for "just plain 'bull.'" Aaron studied the maps and wrote out orders by the light of a Coleman lantern. He slept in a cold sleeping bag in a succession of cold houses, all of which reeked of cow manure.

As November drew to a close, the entire cavalry group finally was inside Germany and up against the Switchline when they heard a rumor that the German 11th Panzer Division waited for them north of the Switchline or possibly even south of it.

As the calendar turned to December, the weather grew colder and more inclement. Patrols went out daily to try to capture prisoners and ascertain if enemy units were moving toward them. The weather prevented aerial reconnaissance, but there had been no sign of the Panzers on the ground. Believing the Germans to be too weak to try a large offensive thrust, the Allies settled into a rather quiet war. Little did they know that German high command was then planning a last ditch, all out effort to rout the American forces.

On the morning of 16 December, the Germans began their mighty Ardennes Offensive, known today as the Battle of the Bulge. The 3d Cavalry was located about thirty miles south of the Battle of Echternach on the morning the offensive began. Aaron could hear the cannons clearly as he rode to the headquarters of his old unit, the 4th Infantry Division, to borrow field artillery to clear Germans within the Saar-Moselle Triangle.

When he arrived, he found "everybody was running around like crazy." He couldn't figure out why. Before he had left, a pal from the 4th had told him by radio that they hadn't heard an artillery round from the enemy in weeks, and they were glad to have the rest. But three to four German divisions pummeled the 4th Infantry Division at once, and every able-bodied man rushed to the front with an M-1 rifle, even the cooks and the soldiers in the band.

Cohn hurried back to his command post in France on the 4th Division's southern flank, knowing that "pretty soon there would be hell to pay." He told Colonel Polk, "Sir, I couldn't get any artillery. They're fighting like hell up there." And that is how Jimmy Polk learned of the Battle of the Bulge.

Across the river, Cohn could see activity. There were rumors that they would be facing the 11th Panzer Division sooner or later. That meant that their two squadrons of fifteen hundred men would be facing sixteen thousand elite troops.

At eleven that night, Colonel Polk got a call from XX Corps. They had decoded Fieldmarshal Von Rundstedt's radio orders dispatching the 11th Division down through the Saar-Moselle Triangle. The Panzer division was going to hit the 3d Cavalry "right on the nose the first thing in the morning." Polk asked the caller what help headquarters would be sending. The officer responded that the corps had nothing to offer them. They were on their own. Polk told the man, "Well, you'd better get headquarters mobile then, because there is no way the 3d Cavalry can hold off a Panzer division."

Polk decided not to divulge this information to anyone. He "knew it would scare them to death." Because of his discretion, Aaron got a relatively good night's sleep. And the next morning Polk discovered that luck was on their side.

The XX Corps command later learned that Adolph Hitler himself countermanded the field marshal's order because he did not want the girth of the German bulge in Allied lines to be enlarged any further. So, after joining the war to "shoot Hitler himself," Aaron now had Hitler to thank for sparing his life.

Through the coldest weeks of the winter, the 3d Cavalry sat stalled behind the fortifications of the Switchline and the Siegfried Line as the Battle of the Bulge raged on. On 22 December Lt. Gen. George S. Patton Jr. wrote a Christmas card to his men in the field and had it disbursed to the entire Third Army. It gave everyone an extra measure of courage to read these words: "I have full confidence in your courage, devotion to duty, and skill in battle. We march in our might to complete victory. May God's blessing rest upon each of you on this Christmas Day." On the other side of the wallet-sized, brown card was printed a prayer written by the Third Army chaplain, asking for the clouds to lift so that the air forces could be used to relieve the siege at Bastogne.

"Almighty and most merciful father, we humbly beseech thee, of thy great goodness, to restrain these immoderate rains with which we have had to contend. Grant us fair weather for battle. Graciously hearken to us as soldiers who call thee that, armed with thy power, we may advance from victory to victory and crush the oppression and wickedness of our enemies, and establish thy justice among men and nations. Amen."

On December 23rd Aaron attended a meeting at the headquarters of the 10th Armored Division where he was going to brief an officer of the 10th who was also involved in reconnaissance—from the air. When Aaron saw that the man was none other than Mulford "Mutt" Jordan of Columbus, he was delighted, and they had a warm reunion. Aaron showed Mutt his reconnaissance map, pointing out where the enemy had dug in. The next day, Christmas Eve, Jordan was flying another reconnaissance mission when his plane was shot down, and he perished.

That same day General Walker of XX Corps decided to address an assembly of men, whom Aaron made sure were assembled at their command post at Sierck on the river. The crowd stood waiting for General Walker, but just before he arrived, a half dozen P-47s strafed them, killing twenty-six men, seriously wounding three, and burning several trucks. This blow hurt even more when they learned that inexperienced American pilots who had mistaken the river lines had done the killing.

In spite of the tragedy and the inevitable homesickness caused by being in a war on the other side of the world from loved ones on yet another holiday, many of the front line troops maintained good spirits. They appointed their gun positions with Christmas trees decorated with looted German ornaments.

Everyone ate turkey on the twenty-fifth. At one location the men picked up instruments from around town and improvised an orchestra to play Christmas music. At headquarters, Aaron ate his turkey with cranberry sauce that had been mailed to the colonel by one of his family members. The sun reflecting off the snow made this cold day a bright one. The staff observed a meaningful outdoor Christmas service at a wayside cross. They sang Christmas carols, with Aaron's voice as loud as the rest of them. Then they walked inside to down a few drinks and "try to be happy, but it was mighty hard going," wrote the colonel to his wife.

Aaron thought little of Chanukah during the war. There

was no Jewish chaplain around, and what little time there was to observe a religious service, he gladly supported whatever faith was represented, and he was proud to celebrate Christmas with his comrades. One of his dearest friends was the Catholic chaplain, Fr. George Brennan. Whenever the padre wished to conduct a service, Aaron helped him set a time and place for it. And Aaron told Brennan that if he were ever in need of it, he wanted Brennan to perform last rites for him.

On 26 December, the 37th Tank Battalion of the 4th Armored Division reached Bastogne, ending the German siege on that city and marking the beginning of the end for the Nazi army. Throughout the winter Janet Ann sent Aaron packages of wurst, bologna, and sardines with loaves of bread. Aaron shared it all with his crew. He also shared his monthly "Nafi ration," a ration of alcohol given to officers.

By swapping a bottle of scotch for two bottles of gin and acquiring some grape juice, he could give his gun crew a well-

In Luxembourg, Aaron (second from right) and the Third Cavalry Group staff plan their next move.

deserved party. "Rank didn't mean a damn thing" to Aaron by then. He knew they had a job to do, and the best way to do that job was to curry a friendship with the enlisted men and show them that he had their best interest at heart. At the same time he expected every man to do his duty for his unit in "the good old Army way."

North of him in the Ardennes Forest of Belgium and Luxembourg, the Battle of the Bulge continued for several more weeks. Meanwhile, for an interminable two more months of winter, the 3d Cavalry sat at the Siegfried Line. The front line was eerily quiet most of the time, with only the occasional burst of machine gun fire to break the monotony. It was hard on the cavalry to sit in place. They were meant for swift movement to encircle the enemy, not for sitting in foxholes like the infantry. Consumed with the desire to get this war over with, the days dragged past. They envied the Russians who were on the move on the western front.

Colonel Polk wrote on 1 February 1945, "If we could just shake out of this area into the open, past all these dreadful pill boxes, and get going again, I think we all would be happy. But now it looks like a slow process of grinding away until the sudden crack-up comes, and we are rolling again."

CHAPTER 10

"ICH BIN EIN AMERIKANISCHER JUDE!"

The cavalry finally got its wish to be on the move when better visibility allowed tank destroyers to knock out the pill boxes abandoned by the evacuating enemy. Warmer weather also cleared some of the mud and snow to allow freer movement altogether. At last the Luftwaffe had been knocked out of the sky, and the Allies had air supremacy.

By the first of March 1945, the 3d Cavalry was crossing the Saar River and breaking through the Siegfried Line. During the next two days some elements of the squadrons crossed the river at several bridgeheads then turned northeast toward Trier, which had been captured by the 10th Armored and the 94th Divisions.

The Brave Rifles took up a position on the north flank of XX Corps between the Moselle River and the city of Trier. The squadrons encountered pockets of resistance when the enemy "attacked . . . with startling force, as if they were furious that we had taken Trier away from them."[10]

Colonel Polk wrote home. "The roads were littered with burned-out tanks, trucks and things that men throw away in a precipitous retreat." He also wrote of the relief he experienced in getting past the Siegfried Line at long last: "It is wonderful to get away from the stink of it into fresh air and the absence of mines."

The 3d Cavalry Group next was ordered into the Palatinate, the region between the Saar and Rhine Rivers. They found this region mobbed with traffic as the Third and Seventh Armies converged.

At this time, a request came in from Twelfth Army Group for a field grade officer with combat experience who also was familiar with court-martial procedure. The job's requirements could not have been more tailored to Aaron's experience. Colonel Polk called him over and handed him the request. "I hate to lose you but I've got to show you this," said Polk. "Here's your pass. You'll be well taken care of in the rear."

Aaron read the request and thought, "Here's my ticket to a cushy, safe place in this ugly, old war." But before he had even finished reading the note, he had made up his mind not to take it. Thinking of his buddies whom he'd been with since the beginning of this war, he heaved a sigh and tore the order in two.

"Colonel Polk, you know I could never leave you," he said.

Jimmy Polk smiled broadly. He had only been testing Aaron's loyalty, and he was grateful Cohn had not let him down.

General Patton ordered the Third Army to outflank and surround the Germans in order to cut their supply lines. Without food, gas, or ammunition, the enemy could either surrender or make a run for it. A captured German POW told his interrogators that the only army the Germans feared was the Third Army, especially the elements of the 90th Infantry Division, the 4th Armored Division, and the 3d Cavalry Group. "When any of them appear on our front, we know we are going to get it," he said.

In the Palatinate they also encountered a sight they were not prepared for—thousands of freed slave laborers. Wrote Technical Sergeant Joe Radanovich of the 3d Squadron, "The roads were choked with all kinds of people: Russians, Slavs, Poles, Italians, every kind of nationality in Europe, and every one with a big smile on his face. It must be a fine feeling to be freed from Hitler and his monsters."

Colonel Polk mentioned these released laborers in his letter home on 23 March.

> If you could see the released slave labor we have
> freed, Russians, Poles, Czechs, Italians, French,
> all completely starved and tattered. All taking to
> the highways to get home after five bitter years.
> They are pitiful and terrible creatures—men,
> women, and children as released slaves. And the
> Germans fear them as well they might, for they
> will steal and kill to eat, rape to satisfy their lust.
> We are collecting them to feed them and get
> them to the Red Cross, but as yet they are like
> wild things, like animals released from pens who
> will not be penned again. They beg any kind of
> food and wolf it down . . . while the German
> people are fat . . . When we first capture a town,
> [the Germans] put out white flags and then
> wave and line the streets like it was a parade. It
> is a beautiful country, but filled with wreckage
> and human sorrow. The crime of this slave labor
> stinks up the whole world, this crime that the
> Germans can never pay enough for.

On 23 March 1945, the 3d Cavalry staff and headquarters troop were "installed in a nice row of six houses, all modern." Polk wrote home, "We just marched up and gave the people fifteen minutes to leave. We didn't give a damn where they went, just get out . . . Does it seem cruel? Damn them all, they have it coming."

The war continued. One night as the Americans held a piece of high ground, the Germans counter attacked. When Aaron notified Colonel Polk, the CO said, "Show me on the map where they are." Cohn did just that, and Polk scratched his weary head. "Hell, if that's where they are, they're right on top of us."

"Yes sir," said Major Cohn. "Come to the window, and I'll

show you."

Half a mile away they could see the tank battle, and Polk snarled, "Why didn't you show me this to begin with?"

"Sir, you insisted I show it to you on the map."

The Palatinate remained congested. Truckloads of German prisoners headed east while Aaron's group waited for their turn to cross the bridges over the Rhine. General Polk wrote, "It isn't like those lean days of last summer and fall, when there were few troops and short rations and damn little ammunition. Now there is everything; all sorts of troops crowding each other to get over the bridges, all sorts of everything crowding up. The spirit of everyone is a joy to behold. We know we are in the greatest Army in the world, the 'Mighty 3d,' that nothing can stop us."

The Third Army stood out as defiantly different from the other allied forces in Germany. Never obeying the speed limits, they were often seen whooping it up as they sped down the road "loaded down with ammunition and in a hell of a hurry." Colonel Polk wrote that theirs was "a very proud army," and he said, "it would break our hearts to ever get shifted over to some other one."

They were moving swiftly now. They crossed the Rhine River on Aaron's twenty-ninth birthday, 3 March 1945, then the 3d Cavalry moved out to lead XX Corps again, driving northeast just above Frankfurt, then turning north. In two days they covered another seventy miles. When they hit the Fulda River at Bebra and Rotenburg, they "got in a scrap" before capturing both towns. At Kassel they encircled three sides of the town while the infantry captured it from the north. From what Aaron saw of the center of that city, there was nothing left of it but a brick pile.

After Kassel, they turned due east toward Chemnitz. The XX Corps was now in a box formation with the armored divisions leading, the Cavalry on the flanks, and the infantry cleaning up the rear. The countryside was beautiful to behold, and their work was relatively easy as they crossed Germany in the direction of Czechoslovakia.

Although Germans were surrendering by the carload now,

Polk explained in a letter home that they never knew when they would "run into a bunch of fanatics and all of a sudden, it's just a hell of a fight." As Aaron put it, by May 1945 the Germans he encountered "were either at your feet or at your throat." General Polk's summation of this final action of the war shows how the cavalry and infantry interfaced.

> From Kassel we went east past Gera, Jena, and Weimar near Chemnitz. It was nice as we had an armored division on each side of us and we really knocked them over. Then the Third Army turned south and we moved from one flank of the Army to the other, made a long march behind the lines and wound up south of Nuremberg. Next, we jumped out in front again and were announced as an armored division of Third Army, driving on Regensburg. We hit the Danube, stopped while the Infantry came up and forced a crossing over the River, then moved out in front again and fought our way down to Braunau on the Inn River. It was a short wait again while the infantry got across and we were off into Austria.

Polk wrote that the drive from Nuremberg down to the Danube River at Regensburg "really was amazingly good. We were, at times, thirty miles out in front of anyone and all by ourselves. In three days, we captured 1,400 prisoners, untold warehouses, railroad trains and everything you can think of. And with it all, we had about nine casualties . . . (hurt, not killed). I really am proud of this outfit. The Corps and Army Commanders both sent a 'well done' by radio on this mission."

It was at the Danube that Aaron encountered his former ROTC instructor from UGA. He had taught Cohn at Fort Oglethorpe, and Aaron considered him an old hero. But having just arrived at the front in his first day of combat, his instructor was overwhelmed and nervous as a cat. He was standing in a lead position on the leading vehicle, a posture highly vulnerable and imprudent for a high-ranking officer in a war zone. When Aaron jumped aboard to brief the officer that the 3d Cavalry Group was holding the bridgehead, Aaron was happy to see him, but the officer only snarled at Cohn, "I have no time for you, major. I want to know what's on the other side of the river."

With the timing of a comedian, Major Cohn replied, "Germans, sir."

Aaron met his doubles partner from UGA near the Danube. Joe Hilsman of the 75th Ranger Battalion and Aaron just stared at each other. "What the hell are *you* doing here?" they asked in unison.

Cohn was now spending his days studying the map to figure "where the Russians are, and where the end of Germany is, and how much farther we have to go."

Three days before V-E Day, the infantry crossed into Austria at Braunau on the Inn River. The 3d Cavalry crossed behind them that night. The next morning the cavalry headed off to meet the Russians on the Enns River near Steyr, Austria. Late that same afternoon, they captured an entire Hungarian division. They ran into their last fight near Vocklabruck when they encountered a group of fanatical SS troops. For two hours, they went at each other until the Germans surrendered.

At noon the next day, they reached Steyr, and they ran "right up the back of a German SS Division which had orders to let us through." Wrote Polk, "They were faced in the other direction toward the Russians and it certainly was a spooky feeling to be moving between Krauts armed to the teeth and no truce or peace or anything, just sort of an unwritten agreement. To tell you the truth, I was scared sick, for if anyone had gotten trigger happy, it would have been too bad."

The 3d Cavalry sent patrols across the Enns River, but the Russians were nowhere to be seen. Everyone was disappointed when the infantry relieved them the next day, and they were ordered to return to the Austrian Alps. There they cleaned out pockets of German soldiers that had been bypassed on their first pass through.

These Nazis surrendered without a fight. Aaron rode from one town to another in a machine-gun-mounted jeep amidst Germans with their hands up marching down the roads in the direction of a prisoner of war camp. The Germans were frantic to surrender to the Americans, who they knew would abide by the Geneva Convention protocol as opposed to the Russian army.

Aaron slowed his jeep when he saw a seventeen-year-old German soldier in the road, his hands up in hopes he could surrender to Aaron. Cohn told him he didn't have time. The boy answered in English, "There are 150 soldiers in that village you just passed." They could have ambushed Cohn, but instead they were waiting to surrender to someone. As Aaron and the teenager drove back to the village, he told the lad he spoke German, "so don't double cross me." The boy hollered a phrase in German that informed them an American officer was there. The Germans filed out of a building with their hands in the air and formed a line. At Aaron's command, they threw down their weapons while he fingered his 45-caliber handgun.

Then a prisoner in the front row said in perfect English, "Major, please put that God damned gun down before one of us gets killed."

"Who the hell said that?" asked Aaron.

"I did," replied a man who had been born and reared in Cincinnati. He explained to Aaron how he ended up in the German army: "I was visiting my mother when the war started, and they wouldn't let me go back to the US. They drafted me."

"Well, you take these lunk heads, line them up in columns of four. There's a POW camp right down the road. March them down there."

On 7 May Cohn and the men of the 3d Cavalry were enjoying the view of a beautiful mountain lake near Seewalchen, Austria. At about one p.m. the radio came to life. The Morse coded message was preceded by a string of Os, indicating highest priority and urgency. General Dwight D. Eisenhower's message announced that German high command had signed an unconditional surrender, and a cease-fire would begin at midnight on 9 May. The message center personnel called out the news to great "whoops and shouts."

That night the officers made "atomic punch" with any kind of spirits they could lay their hands on, all mixed together. Although they were joyous the war in Europe was ending, the ongoing war against Japan prevented full-scale revelry. They wondered if they next would be going to the Pacific. Aaron's mind also was consumed by the horrendous sight he had witnessed the day before, on 6 May.

He had been driving near Seewalchen, Austria, near the crystal blue lakes and white-capped spires of the Austrian Alps following close behind one of the 3d Cav tanks (of F Company, 3d Squadron commanded by his friend Tim Brennan) when Cohn's jeep pulled up at the gate of a concentration camp. Although he already had encountered the Ohdruf concentration camp, Ebensee, a satellite camp of the more well-known camp at Mauthausen, was a shock to him. The Americans had no prior knowledge of Ebensee, which housed eighteen thousand prisoners representing fifteen different nationalities.

A barbed wire electric fence surrounded the compound on the outskirts of a small town. The Germans, who had stood in the watch towers with machine guns trained inward, had vanished minutes before the first American tanks rolled up. When the cavalry radioed to headquarters to report what they'd found, Polk knew Aaron would want to be there. He told Major Cohn to drive to the camp immediately.

The inmates had heard airplanes flying high overhead for a few weeks, and in the evenings they had heard artillery fire, so they assumed the Allies were closing in on the Germans. An orphaned teenager by the name of Eliezer Ayalon smiled to himself as he spied a red flame on the night horizon. In the last days of the war, the starving inmates had been reduced to eating leaves and any other greenery they could find as they walked from the camp to the nearby tunnels where they worked each day.

To Ayalon who had been at this camp only a few weeks, there seemed to be little difference between the living and the dead. One of his friends awoke in horror to find he was lying in the middle of a pile of naked skeletons on their way to the crematorium. The boy had been mistaken for dead when he fainted, and the guards had tossed him onto the heap of discarded lives.

Hours before Aaron Cohn arrived at the gates of Ebensee, the German guards had ordered the inmates to walk into the tunnels. The prisoners knew from underground intelligence that the Germans intended to obliterate any sign of the camp by luring them into the tunnels and then exploding them. When the camp commandant told the crowd that the Americans were coming and their only chance of survival was to hide in the tunnels, the people in their many different languages shouted, "No!" The German SS officers then turned and walked out of the camp to save themselves.[11]

A few hours later, Aaron found the gates of Ebensee open. He strode into the compound with his steel helmet covering his blonde hair and shading his freckled face. With his breeches tucked inside his knee-length tank boots, Aaron carried a forty-five automatic pistol in its shoulder holster over his left breast.

The stench of the place was the first thing to assault him. Then his eyes beheld the huge pile of naked cadavers. He estimated there were at least five hundred corpses rotting in the courtyard, eyes and mouths open to the heavens in silent screams while maggots and flies crawled over them.

Next, Aaron took in the crowd of about one hundred survivors standing before him. Some were dressed in shabby gray striped uniforms. Some were naked. It was hard not to stare at them. Their swollen knees and testicles, contrasting with their otherwise skeleton-like appearance, spoke volumes about the enforced starvation they had suffered. They looked like "bones, covered in yellow skin."[12] Their average weight was seventy pounds.

Noting the way Aaron was dressed, one of the prisoners whispered to the others in German, "That is an SS officer." The crowd shrunk back in fear. They had seen all too many of the SS troops, charged with the genocide and extermination of the Jews of Europe in Hitler's "final solution."

Looking into their gaunt faces, Aaron reassured them that he was not a German trooper; he was an American Major.

Aaron held his breath as the human corpses inched toward him in relief. Then he told them the proudest part of who he

This concentration camp photo appeared in *The XX Corps: Its History and Service in World War II.*

was. "Ich bin ein amerikanischer Jude!" He was Jewish! With tears of relief, the crowd kissed and hugged him. Their demonic nightmare was at last over. And a member of their own faith had saved them.

They all began talking at once. "Do you know my Uncle Lou in San Francisco? How about my Aunt Sadie in Brooklyn? I have a cousin in St. Louis!"

For Aaron this joyous moment represented a perfect culmination of his months of war now virtually behind him. He had come to Europe to liberate Jews from the mistreatment of the Nazis, and here he stood, a personal liberator to a band of pitiable prisoners whose only crime had been their religion.

Some of the prisoners showed Aaron around the compound. He found seven two-story wooden buildings that housed the

This photo of the liberation of the camp at Ebensee was published in *The XX Corps: Its History and Service in World War II.*

workers. Forced to build an underground factory in the Alps and fed very little, Jews and Gentiles from such varied homelands as Russia, Czechoslovakia, Poland, France, Greece, and Germany had grown weaker over time. As their health declined, their captors organized their sleeping quarters according to their strength, moving them to the next bunkhouse as they grew weaker. The last building lay only a few yards from a crematorium, making it easy for the Germans to dispose of their bodies. In building seven, Aaron found barely-breathing human skeletons, lying in their own excrement.

In spite of the German army's brutal efficiency, the crematorium staff had been unable to deal with the sheer numbers of people "dying in the hospital, in the barracks, on the fields, between the barracks, on the roads." Even though it ran twenty-four hours a day and burned eight corpses at a time, they could not handle the rate of the dying. The prisoners themselves had been ordered to collect the corpses for burning twice daily to prevent cannibalism. But in its last few weeks in operation, they had begun digging ditches beyond the camp and dropping them in "like logs for burning." Then the Germans learned of the cease-fire and fled. Some inmates showed him the railroad ties where several at a time were forced to lie down before being shot to death, then burned en masse on the railroad ties.

When Aaron arrived at Ebensee there were 16,650 registered "healthy" prisoners and another 7,566 listed as ill.[13] Having been treated like animals, they had become such. "They would fight like dogs over a piece of bread and would readily kill for a few potato peelings."[14] Aaron watched in horror as an American soldier dropped a bag of flour. When it split open, six men dove into the mess, licking up the white flour from the black mud.

Among the people Aaron spoke to at Ebensee was a Viennese attorney who kissed his hand and told him he had been decorated personally by the Emperor Franz Joseph for his service in World War I. "And now look at me!" he said. "You must promise me that you will do everything you can when you go back to the US to make sure that no one ever does this to you.

Tell them what you have seen."

Aaron also met a refined and lovely girl who had been educated at one of the best schools in England. She told him how she had been trying on some shoes, and she had one shoe of one kind on and another of a different kind when the Gestapo came and arrested her family, putting her in one work camp, her father in another, her mother in another, and her little brother in yet another camp. She never saw them again. The Germans inadvertently saved her life by placing her in a brothel for German officers. She was sent to Ebensee not long before Aaron found her.

Aaron was sickened to hear how during their incarceration each nationality had kept to itself because of ancient ethnic divisions. There was deep-seated hatred among the people of the Balkan States. The Slovaks and the Croats had been fighting for two-thousand-years; the Poles and the Magyars could not get along. The non-Jews hated the Jews. Instead of banning together to try to survive, they actually had broken apart. One group became the enemy of another. It was hard for Aaron to imagine living like this—like beasts in a wild and deathly kingdom.

With eighteen thousand people in need of immediate food and medical attention, a mobile army unit was dispatched along with convoys of food and an administrative unit to run things. The army organized the production of food for them in the nearby town, but they had to be careful not to give them food that was too rich for their starving organs. Several more died in the coming days, their bodies simply unable to digest food after so long without it.

These victims represented every profession, from doctors and lawyers to artists and musicians, and all walks of life, from cultured men to peasants and criminals. A famous Polish artist asked if he could paint a portrait of Aaron and a few of the other liberators. Aaron told him that he had no time to sit for a portrait, but the grateful man explained he only needed a couple of hours. After procuring for him the best oils that could be found in Austria, Aaron sat for the portrait. This painting was one of

After Aaron took part in the liberation of the Ebensee Concentration Camp, a survivor painted his portrait in little more than an hour.

Aaron's few mementos of war that made it safely home.

Colonel Polk shared Aaron's feelings about being a liberator: "Their joy and gratitude for us makes me feel humble, yet proud that we were the means of their deliverance. Truly, we have been fighting a holy war as our Chaplain has said. Such sights and such tragedy leave little time for rejoicing. I'm simply drained of emotion by it all. The taste of it is still in my mouth."

General Dwight Eisenhower also had spoken of the war as a "great crusade." Although this phrase was meaningless to many, it meant everything to Aaron. This war was both an international conflict and a personal war to him. He was proud to play a role in history and to play a part in the liberation of his brethren. Forever changed by what he had seen, Aaron would keep Ebensee with him for all his days.

CHAPTER 11

WAR'S END

With others taking over the administration of aid to the people of Ebensee, the regimental staff moved on to other details. There was to be a grand party on 19 May 1945, to celebrate the end of the war in Europe and specifically the ninety-ninth anniversary of the organization of the 3d Cavalry. On a lovely hillside General James Polk welcomed such distinguished visitors as Gen. George Patton, Maj. Gen. William Wyman, and Brig. Gen. Holly Maddox. Each of the generals made remarks, then someone read a letter of congratulations by General Walker of the XX Corps. It summarized all that the 3d Cavalry had accomplished since landing in France:

> When the history of the present War in Europe
> is written, no narrative could be complete, no
> account could be either adequate or accurate
> unless it told, and told at some length, of your
> achievements. Of how, during the early part
> of August 1944, August the 10th to be exact,
> while some of you were still en route to join XX
> Corps you received the urgent and very vital
> mission of area reconnaissance from Vitre and
> Angers, seventy-five miles east of Blois. In three

short days and nights you justified our faith and pointed the way for the Infantry-Armor wedge that XX Corps drove between the Fifteenth and Seventh German Armies. Wheeling northeast, the speed and aggressiveness of your thrust to Chartres, then the sudden, bewildering dash straight east that lanced through and behind enemy lines to reach the Seine River, are illustrious pages in the brilliant chapters your deeds have written in this present campaign. First to reach the Meuse River, first on the Moselle River and the first Americans in Thionville, where you struck terror and dismay into the hearts of the German soldiers. In the reduction of Fortress Metz, your efforts contributed as much as any single unit, be it Armor, Infantry, or Artillery in the elimination of the last barrier that stood like a shield to our entry into Germany. In fact, yours were the first troops of XX Corps to enter Germany.

In the development of the Siegfried Line and the Pursuit through the Palatinate, the name of Task Force Polk became synonymous with boldness and aggressiveness. Your 150-mile dash in three days from the Rhine River to the Fulda River, when you permitted an entire infantry division to be motorized and moved forward without detrucking, was one of the most important and significant tactical achievements of this entire war. Of how, finally in the concluding days of this campaign you acted as a special Combat Team for the Corps Commander. Your execution of this mission was done with all the dash and daring of Stuart's Famous Raiders themselves . . . I can think of no more fitting

tribute or toast to you, than to echo the words of
General Winfield Scott, which were addressed
to the 3d Cavalry, when he saw our National
Flag erected above Chapultepec by one of your
fellow 3d Cavalrymen, and this I quote, 'Brave
rifles, veterans, you have been baptized in fire
and blood and have come out steel.

General Patton awarded Polk the Oakleaf Cluster to the
Silver Star Medal "for outstanding leadership of an outstanding
unit." All the men of this "outstanding unit" cheered their
leader, and many were close to tears with pride in what they had
accomplished together and what they had survived.

Although Aaron was enjoying a three-day vacation in Paris
at this time, at the insistence of Colonel Polk, his thoughts also
drifted back to reflect on what the war had accomplished. Back at
Fort Benning in 1940, the Inspector General of the 4th Infantry
Division had lectured Aaron about the superiority of the Regular
Army over the Citizen Army, which he believed never could
be effective. Hitler also had considered the army of America,
a "mongrel nation," to be a poor substitute for the German
nation's. When Aaron thought of all he had experienced since
D-Day with these men of the Brave Rifles he was humbled. These
young citizen soldiers of the USA, descendants of many different
backgrounds, ethnic groups, and religions, had turned out to be
great soldiers. By the end of the war one could not tell a West
Pointer from an ROTC graduate. The war had transformed the
American army into the epitome of what American democracy
stands for. Regardless of their race, creed, or color, they were
American soldiers standing tall with self-esteem. Cohn could not
have been prouder.

Americans in Europe wondered when they could go home
or if they would be sent to the Pacific. A point system for the
enlisted men allotted so many points for decorations, service, etc.
They weren't sure how officers would be treated at that moment,
but it turned out that Aaron had earned enough points to be one

Soon after Germany surrendered, Colonel Polk gave Major Cohn a much-deserved three-day leave to see Paris for the first time.

of the first groups of officers to return stateside. As a "high point man," he would be leaving Europe in a few months.

In the meantime, the Third Army command had reason to believe Tito and his guerillas were marching up into the American sector of occupation from the south, and they ordered the 3d Cavalry to stop them. Although Tito was not there, they did encounter in crossing the Italian Alps like Hannibal of old their first terrain better suited for horses than tanks. On this steep terrain with a gorge to their immediate right and a steep incline to the left, if the enemy had met them here on horseback, the

Americans would have been sitting ducks. Luckily, the only army they found in the vicinity were elements of the British Eighth Army as they moved north from Italy.

One day there came a knock at the door of the command post. A British officer said to Aaron, "My colonel would like to see your colonel at our headquarters."

Since Polk was a full colonel and Aaron ascertained the British officer was a lieutenant colonel, Polk sent Aaron to the meeting. Cohn arrived at tea time, and he was not asked to join them. He waited for some time before they finally got around to the purpose of the meeting. The British commander told him how a fellow American officer from the 3rd Squadron had taken a horse away from a German major who had been acting like a conqueror, victoriously riding in the American bivouac area as though he had won the war. Aaron's friend had told him to dismount, and the German had replied that the British had given him permission to ride the horse.

Aaron's friend's then shouted, "Get the hell off that horse, or I'll shoot you off of it."

The German complained to the British, and the British lieutenant colonel complained to Aaron that the Americans were "mucking things up."

Aaron's eyes grew cold. He pointed his finger at the Brit and told him this war had been no soccer game for the 3d Cavalry. "We lost dear comrades to come over here and beat the hell out of Hitler. The horse was a booty of war, and we will not let a defeated enemy act this way. You have no jurisdiction over us." Cohn saluted and stomped out. He drove back to his command post and told Colonel Polk word for word what he had said on his behalf. Polk agreed with all of it.

The 3d Cavalry's next assignment was to serve as an occupation army in Bavaria, in the southeastern region of Germany, to stabilize the war-torn area. It was a very sad day, indeed, when in June 1945 Aaron Cohn said farewell to his hero, Jimmy Polk, to become the ranking officer of the armored section of XX Corps. Aaron spent the summer of 1945 in Bavaria.

One day as he walked down a road not far from headquarters, he spied two red clay tennis courts behind a private home. Aaron had not played tennis since his Camp Gordon days before the war, and the site of the courts filled him with longing. As he stood there, an old man approached him and asked, "Spielen Sie Tennis?"

Standing before Aaron was Bino Siedhof, who had coached some of the finest women players in Germany for the acclaimed international competition known as the "Federation Cup." Bino had a sister, Ruth Weiss, and a lovely fifteen-year-old niece named Jubilate, who became his friend for life. (They would visit each other after the war in Regensburg, Paris, and Columbus.)

Aaron and Bino began playing tennis regularly and became close friends. Aaron could not help but notice the privations the Siedhof family endured because of the war. He began bringing them food when he came for tennis.

One day when Bino's nephew Rainier was playing, he picked up a hand grenade, and it exploded, severely injuring the boy's hand. Aaron got hold of an army vehicle and rushed Rainier to a German military hospital. But a German medical official denied the boy treatment because he was not a military dependent.

Aaron raised up to full height and told the intake officer that he *would* take care of this child, or Aaron would shoot him. "We did not wage war against old people and children," he said.

The German captain decided to report Aaron for his conduct. Aaron said that was fine with him. When the officer asked his name, Aaron proudly told him. Upon hearing Aaron's last name, the German quickly changed his mind and found medical attention for the boy who was able to recover well from his wound.

Because of such tender care on Aaron's part, the Weiss-Siedhof family considered Aaron to be "a humanitarian, not a conqueror." And Aaron loved this family as though they were his own.

Eventually Siedhof introduced him to the Baron Gottfried

Von Cramm, one of the most celebrated players in Europe who had played on the German's Davis Cup team before the war (and who later married Barbara Hutton). Von Cramm was known as an honorable player. He once lost a match point at Wimbledon when he admitted his racket touched the ball before it was called out. One glorious afternoon, ten players met at the Siedhof's courts for some convivial tennis, and to Aaron's delight, he played a set against Von Cramm. Even though Aaron lost 4:6, he had to pinch himself to believe his luck at meeting and playing with such a distinguished opponent.

Cohn did not return home with the 3d Cavalry per se. On his returning LST were guys from every division in the war. Officers bunked on the upper deck. Enlisted men bunked below. Every day of the crossing, the recreation officer set up a boxing ring on the lower deck, and the enlisted men began to sound off to the officers, "Do any of you chicken shit officers want to fight?"

Aaron noted the anger in their voices. Although he had never treated his men with disrespect, some officers had belittled their men, and it was obvious they were tired of the mistreatment. Four days passed at sea, and every day the men called up to the "chicken shit officers" to challenge them to fight. On day five, Aaron had enough of the enlisted men's conduct. He said he'd fight the sergeant waiting in the ring below.

The crowd whooped and hollered, "We got a major! We got a major!"

Major Cohn peeled off his shirt and climbed into the ring. The boxers went after each other with all the pent up rage they'd stored from their war experience. They pummeled each other until both were bloody.

When the fight was called, the sergeant hugged Aaron in congratulations. "You are one helluva guy," he said. Aaron's fierceness put an end to the insulting cat calls.

Aaron received two cartons of cigarettes as a prize. He opened the cartons and threw cigarettes out to the now friendly crowd remembering the fight he won in Columbus so many years ago when someone had yelled, "Kill that Jew boy!"

Once again, being an aggressive competitor had been the best defense against discrimination of any kind.

Iwo Jima Eulogy

Fifteen hundred Jewish Marines fought in the Battle of Iwo Jima. Rabbi Roland B. Gittlesohn, the first Jewish chaplain of the Marine Corps, ministered to many of the six thousand fallen soldiers of every faith. After the battle was won, Gittlesohn delivered a short eulogy to a small, segregated memorial service because of the prejudice of some Christian chaplains. But unbeknownst to Gittlesohn, three sympathetic Christian chaplains disseminated his text, leading to an avalanche of press coverage that caused the eulogy to be published broadly in America.

When Aaron Cohn read it, he saved a copy in his most cherished papers. Gittleson's words expressed everything that Cohn believed in as a first-generation American and all that he had witnessed as a soldier in the American army—a citizen army where men from all walks of life and representing every religion, creed, and color had fought side-by-side.

Here lie men who loved America because
their ancestors generations ago helped in her
founding, and other men who loved her with
equal passion because they themselves or
their own fathers escaped from oppression to
her blessed shores. Here lie officers and men,
Negroes and whites, rich men and poor . . .
together. Here are Protestants, Catholics and

Jews together. Here no man prefers another because of his faith or despises him because of his color. Here there are no quotas of how many men of each group are admitted or allowed. Among these men there is no discrimination. No prejudices. No hatred. Theirs is the highest and purest democracy. Whosoever of us lifts his hand in hate against a brother, or who thinks himself superior to those who happen to be in the minority, makes of this ceremony and the bloody sacrifice it commemorates, an empty, hollow mockery. To this, then, as our solemn duty, sacred duty do we the living now dedicate ourselves: to the right of Protestants, Catholics and Jews, of white men and Negroes alike, to enjoy the democracy for which all of them have here paid the price . . . We here solemnly swear that this shall not be in vain. Out of this and from the suffering and sorrow of those who mourn this will come, we promise, the birth of a new freedom for the sons of men everywhere.

CHAPTER 12

FAMILY MAN

After serving in an elite combat unit in one of America's greatest armies, Aaron returned to his family in October 1945. It seemed surreal to be meeting Janet Ann on the same Camp Gordon corner where they had parted in the spring of 1944. This year and a half of war had changed Aaron. He was leaner and harder.

After witnessing the fate of those dead and dying victims of Ebensee, he never would be the same. And knowing that one million children had died at the hands of the Nazis caused him to see children differently. For what future does a nation have without the flower of its society to mature into tomorrow's leaders?

Like many Americans, Aaron and Janet Ann had made great sacrifices for their country. The war had taken Janet Ann's brother, several of Aaron's closest army friends, and much of the Cohn family farm. But all they could do now was to put the pieces of their lives back together again and move forward.

They celebrated Aaron's homecoming with lunch at the Partridge Inn. As he savored his first meal of southern comfort food in months, he told Janet Ann about the state of affairs on the other side of the Atlantic.

"Europe will never be the same . . . Hatred, hatred, hatred . . .

I wouldn't live in Europe if they gave me the whole continent."

Janet Ann waited for Aaron to clean his plate, then she asked him coyly, "Well, Aaron, what do you want *now*?"

Without a second's hesitation Aaron said, "I want a milk shake."

Janet Ann snickered. She knew how much Aaron had always loved milk shakes. In Europe after the armistice, he once stood in line for two hours just to get one.

Although Aaron was leaving active duty as a lieutenant colonel, he remained in the Army Reserves for nineteen more years, becoming a colonel in 1958. Until he retired in 1965 with twenty-seven total years of service, he spent one weekend per month and two weeks each summer away from his family, training.

Once he was back in Columbus Aaron thanked God every day for returning him from war to the city he loved, located, as far as he was concerned, in the best nation on Earth. He vowed to return to Fort Benning every year to tell the young officers what he had seen in Ebensee in hopes that he could in some small way prevent something like that from ever happening again. He also made himself available to speak to churches and synagogues about the atrocities of the Holocaust. However, he received few invitations. It seemed most people didn't want to believe that fellow humans—even their former enemy—could be capable of such diabolical acts.

"My synagogue didn't want to talk about it. The temple didn't want to talk about it. Nobody wanted to talk about it. Nobody," said Aaron.

Only after the space of many years had distanced them from the war would they be ready to hear Aaron's story. Occasionally Aaron had nightmares in which he watched as his comrades in arms died all over again. He could have become embittered by what he had witnessed or by the way Americans were turning their backs on what happened to his people, but instead he became even more patriotic.

He loved his country with all his heart. He had volunteered

to fight for her in combat, and now that he was home, he intended to make a contribution to her future. As far as he was concerned it was "pay back time" to the nation that had given his family a second chance forty years earlier.

As a Jewish American Aaron was a staunch supporter of the new state of Israel, which he saw as being analogous to the plight of Irish Americans of old who had supported an Irish free state. But he found that some of his friends at the temple were not inclined to support the world's first modern Jewish state, even though it aspired to be a haven to oppressed people of every land.

Sometimes their lack of sensitivity caused him to explode in frustration, "Your problem is that you didn't see what I saw. Your problem is that you have never lost anybody due to such atrocities. Your problem is that you've lived in a nice, safe place all your life, and you just can't imagine what hell those people have suffered."

But for the most part, Aaron held his peace. His experiences had made him more appreciative of the diversity of religions in his beloved country and the need to respect the rights of those who did not agree with him, for such was the historical foundation that had made his country so great. Aaron focused on whatever positive acts he could accomplish to make the world a better place. After all, this was the essence of Judeo-Christian teachings.

Until Aaron could afford to buy his family their first home, the Cohns lived with the Lilienthals. Gail, now two years old, considered Aaron a stranger and Leslie Lilienthal Sr. her father. While Aaron had been in Europe, she had kissed his picture every night, and now that he was home she continued to "kiss Papa," but she didn't grasp that the man in the picture was the same man that now stood before her waiting to take his place as the most important man in her life. Although it saddened Aaron, he was patient with her.

Aaron yearned for a house of his own, but his adopted parents, the Lilienthals, opened their home and their lives to him,

The Cohns' daughter,
Gail, was born while
Aaron attended
Command General
Staff School at Fort
Leavenworth, Kansas
in 1943.

and he dearly returned their affections. They had lost their one and only son in the war, but if anyone could have stood in Sonny's shadow and thrived, Aaron was that man. The Lilienthals considered bringing Sonny's remains home from Europe, but Aaron was adamant that his bones stay interred in the hallowed ground of the American cemetery in Brittany.

"I want the whole world to know that our family epitomizes patriotism to this great land," he said. "And in death Sonny can inspire others. He can show that diversity and patriotism mingled together can be a beautiful thing."

At last he convinced them, and Sonny's remains are found in the Brittany American Cemetery in Plot One, Row Five, between a soldier from Arkansas and a young man from Texas—a Star of David between two crosses.

"That is what this country is all about," Aaron reminded them.

Eager to get back to his legal work, Aaron was disappointed to learn that his former mentor, George C. Palmer, had died. Leslie Lilienthal hoped Aaron would take Sonny's place as his heir apparent in the management of the Kayser-Lilienthal store. Wherever they went, Leslie never failed to introduce Aaron as his son, not his son-in-law. Out of respect and gratitude and perhaps some survivor's guilt, Aaron considered going into the ladies garment business to please his father-in-law. The advantages were many. His future would be assured, and in the meantime he would earn a nice salary.

But selling women's clothes was the furthest thing from Aaron's mind. He tried to tell Leslie that there were no merchants in his family, implying he wanted to keep it that way. But Leslie asked him just to try it for a while.

Aaron relented, but his heart wasn't in it. His sales technique fell a bit short of the mark. When a woman asked him, "How do you like this dress on me?" he told her: "If *you* like it, buy it. If not, someone else will." The woman thought Aaron had a refreshing sales approach and bought the dress. Even so, Aaron felt like a fish out of water when waiting on women. He couldn't wait for the doors to close each day. After a few days of trying to fit into this new and alien culture, Aaron told Leslie, "Dad, listen. I don't think this is for me."

Leslie begged, "Please, just stay here a little while until you get your feet on the ground." Again, Aaron conceded, but when he overheard women talking about "silly insignificant things," after he had witnessed the concentration camps and the war, such triviality disgusted him.

He told Janet Ann, "Honey, I can't stay in that store. I am going to practice law where I can help people. I think that is what my life is going to be all about."

So Janet Ann told her father, "Please, Dad, turn Aaron

loose." Leslie did, and Aaron gratefully left the clothing business to hang up his shingle.

Early in 1946, with two dependants and another soon to be on the way, Aaron shared an office with his cousin, Aaron Satlof, an amiable man known more for his personality than his scholarship. Once the gold lettering proclaiming "Aaron Cohn, Attorney at Law" was painted on the Eleventh Street window of his second story office in the First National Bank Building (popularly known as the "White Bank Building"), his next objective was to find some clients to allow him to support his family.

Many days there was little to do but wait for clients to darken his door. Sometimes when Janet Ann stopped by with Gail, he was free to take his little girl to Davison's Department Store where customers could check out books. Aaron sometimes spent the last few hours of the day sweltering in his un-air conditioned closet of an office, reading a book by the light beaming down from a sky light—the only source of light in the room.

The clients who did hire Aaron were not of the well-established older generation who already had made their legal connections. Of his prospective client pool, many were shy about using a Jewish attorney for fear that fact would handicap them in court because of prejudice. So half of his early clientele were young black men, many of whom, like Aaron, recently had returned from the war. His other clients were young, white businessmen of Aaron's generation who needed help with their problems.

Cohn enjoyed running title searches, but he found it difficult to get this kind of work because the lending institutions relied on their own stable of established lawyers. Aaron was not too proud to accept any honest work—adoptions, criminal trials, and corporate work. The only work he refused was that which required him to play the devil's advocate. He cared more about sleeping well than making a lot of money. His main source of income came from collecting delinquent debts for a credit bureau.

And, like the other young attorneys in town, he did a lot of pro bono work.

In defending African American clients Aaron quickly became disenchanted with criminal work as he saw first-hand just how unjust a legal system that used "whites only" juries could be. One of his most interesting cases (which did not earn him a nickel) involved a ruptured African American church. With two sets of deacons and two preachers both claiming the same property, one side hired Aaron to help it prevail.

Cohn could see that going to trial would be a waste of time and money, so he called a meeting of both sides, and he asked the members, "Are you going to go down to the courthouse and let that white jury know you can't run your own church? I'll be back in an hour and a half, and I expect there to be *one* preacher, *one* set of deacons, and everyone to be acting like good Christians." That was that.

Every day when Aaron came home from work, Janet Ann asked him tongue-in-cheek, "Did you get a rich client today?" Finally one day, a wealthy member of the temple did call to retain Aaron to speak against a prospective rabbi. Aaron told him he was sorry, but he'd never met the cleric and so could not speak against him.

"Isn't it enough that *I* don't like him?" asked the caller.

"No sir," Aaron replied.

"Then you must be against me," the man said as he slammed down the phone.

That evening Janet Ann asked again, "Did you get a rich client today?"

"Hell no," said Aaron. "Came close. But I'm not sorry."

To supplement his income, Aaron taught history in the evenings at Fort Benning. He also did odd jobs at his father's stockyard to earn an extra ten dollars a week. As the months passed, his law practice began to get busy from word of mouth. Every week Aaron tucked away some money in savings.

In 1947 Aaron was thrilled to welcome into the world his one and only son. Named for the young man the Lilienthals lost to World War II, Leslie Cohn would prove to be his parents' greatest child-rearing challenge.

Aaron's father, Sam, now in his declining years, gave Aaron about as much trouble as Leslie did. Sam had two hundred acres left of his livestock farm on the Macon Road when he abruptly decided to sell it one day. This decision not only was impulsive, it also was imprudent. Aaron counseled him to hold onto the land, which surely would increase in value. With Fort Benning blocking Columbus's development to the south and southeast, the city could only grow in his direction—north and east. Sam's affable nature was ruffled only if someone didn't agree with him, so when Aaron said, "don't," Sam thought "do."

Etta told her husband, "Listen to Aaron!" But Sam had made up his mind. He sold the property, even though it broke his heart to do so, and he began working as a broker at the Columbus stockyard.

Sam's debts began to mount; he became ill; and his estate fell into shambles. Although Aaron never inherited anything from Sam, when Aaron drew up his father's will he found satisfaction in settling Sam's estate without creating acrimony among his siblings.

Sam had many virtues, but Aaron learned more from his father's weaknesses than his strengths. As a consequence Aaron was careful to measure his decisions and heed the counsel of those who were more experienced than he.

Sam was the last of his breed. When he died in 1954 at the age of sixty-seven, on the very night Alabama Attorney General nominee Albert Patterson was shot in Phenix City, all the old livery stables in town had long been closed—gone the way of the horse and buggy.

When Janet Ann became pregnant a third time in 1950, Aaron counted his blessings and hoped for a girl—a sweet, blue-eyed blonde. His prayer was answered to the letter. Jane looked like a little red fish on the day Aaron first met her, but all he saw was her precious beauty. As she grew up, Jane resembled her father more than his other two children. It seemed wherever she went, strangers commented, "You must be Aaron Cohn's child."

Aaron's hope for his daughters' future was that they would make good marriages with men who could provide well for them and that they would raise fine families of good citizens. For Leslie, Aaron envisioned a life much like his own. He hoped to instill in his son a love of athletics, a pride in military service, and a satisfaction in becoming a good, honest attorney and respected civic leader who was known for his integrity. As a consequence, Leslie never considered becoming a fireman or a cowboy when he grew up. He just wanted to be a lawyer like his dad.

At the dinner table, Leslie was the child most likely to need disciplining. But his sisters felt a strong solidarity with him. When Leslie was sent to his room, the girls broke out in tears and stormed upstairs with him.

As the eldest child, Gail became her father's first sergeant. Aaron preceded any commandment to her with "I expect you to . . ." Gail dutifully shouldered the yoke of her father's high standards.

Aaron's military training certainly influenced the way he led his family. He was punctual, dependable, and impatient. Anything worth doing was better done *now*. When he announced that the car would be leaving at 8:30 a.m., the children learned to expect that it might leave even earlier, and if they weren't ready, they'd be left behind (just as Janet Ann had been when she dated Aaron).

Every Friday evening, Aaron arose from the dinner table and said, "I'm going to temple. Would anyone like to come with me?" Even when Gail didn't want to go, she couldn't bear to see her father leave by himself. Her favorite part of the Sabbath service was "a prayer for our country" that began with the words, "Grant us peace, thy most precious gift, O thou eternal source of peace . . . " Then the organist played softly "My Country, 'Tis of Thee." Gail reached for her father's waiting hand at this point in the service. This precious moment constituted her sacred, weekly connection with her dad.

Over the generations, the Cohn family has passed on to their children the faith of their fathers. Here grandfather Aaron and father Leslie take part in grandson Seth's Bar Mitzvah.

Because she loved Aaron, Gail loved her religion. Aaron taught his children that as religious people, they were required by God to do three things as the Prophet Micah had instructed —"to do justly, to love mercy, and to walk humbly with your God." Aaron Cohn not only was his children's religious mentor, he was the Sunday school administrator of the combined schools of Temple Israel and Shearith Israel Synagogue, and he later became president of Temple Israel.

As important as his religion was to him, Aaron also was passionate about bringing people of all faiths together to respect each other. Like an old, black preacher, Cohn wanted to spread his gospel of love to all of God's children. Instead of sitting around and complaining about injustice, becoming bitter because of it, he chose to try and change things.

Aaron combined forces with his best friend, Dr. Seaborn Anderson "Andy" Roddenbery (a Methodist) and Louis Kunze (a Catholic) to hold ecumenical programs around town as a way of breaching the religious divide. Aaron reminded these audiences that Jesus was a rabbi, and the Sermon on the Mount was "pure Judaism." He explained to Christians that members of his faith were not demons. "We're all just flesh and blood like you with similar virtues and flaws."

Cohn became the co-chair of the Columbus Roundtable of the National Council of Christians and Jews, which encouraged more ecumenical gatherings. These included a rare event at the temple when a Catholic Monsignor spoke.

Gail Cohn followed her father from church to church as he presented his programs, and these experiences sparked in her a fascination with comparative religions and a comfort for attending Christian services. Cohn, Roddenbery, and Kunze also hoped that in the near future they could encourage their community to break down racial barriers, but in this regard they were ahead of their time.

Andy Roddenbery, who had been Aaron's close friend since his days on the UGA tennis team, moved next door to Aaron in the 1950s, and their families blended into one extended family. Aaron idolized Andy who was the quintessential All-American guy with a Phi Beta Kappa key and laurels as the captain of the football team. Andy sang at Cohn family weddings, and Aaron spoke at St. Luke Methodist Church at Andy's invitation. When Andy's mother, a devout Catholic, was nearing the end of her life, she insisted that no one but Aaron deliver her eulogy.

Every Sunday after Sunday school, the family ate lunch with the Lilienthals. Afterward, Aaron and the children visited his parents and his aunts and uncles. As the Cohn family members sat in rocking chairs on the front porch, the children listened to their fathers talk about business while the women stayed in the shadows, serving their family and saying little. Jokes and laughter abounded with Aaron as the ringleader, but he also enjoyed serious, intellectual discussions. Family conversations often became animated and passionate, with fingers pointing and hands gesturing.

As Gail grew older she loved to engage her father in similar debates. She sat beside him at the dinner table each evening and soaked up all the attention he had time to give her. She reveled in telling him something he didn't already know. When she was with her father, Gail was never bored.

When Gail told Aaron in the course of one of their passionate debates, "I've heard all that before," Aaron countered by pointing his index finger skyward for emphasis, then saying, "Redundancy is communication."

And when she closed her mind to him, Aaron chided: "People pay for my advice. I'm giving it to you for free!" Or sometimes he'd say, "You're a smart girl. Would you listen to me, please?"

Aaron and his daughter, saw most matters in absolutes in those days. There was right, and there was wrong. Only with age did he begin to see the shades of gray. Jane, the youngest, learned early that "you didn't butt heads with Dad because you didn't win." Yet she also thought her father had very few biases, even for his children. "He was fair without emotion. He was consummately reasonable."

Being the youngest, Jane never got as much time alone with her father as she would have liked. Aaron attended more meetings than most of the town's citizens combined. And when he was home, leaders of various factions called on the telephone or stopped by to speak to him. Aaron's old army friends also came to visit, and the entire family treated these men as returning heroes and dear friends.

Even though Jane occasionally was resentful that her father was not more available to her, she realized even as a youngster that her father had more to give the world than most men. She loved having breakfast alone with him and accompanying him to visit relatives on Sunday afternoons. But Jane's favorite time with her father involved watching war movies together. They both loved "The Guns of Navarone" and "Hell is for Heroes," and Jane would adore war movies even into adulthood because they reminded her of her father, her personal war hero.

As a teenager, Jane was required to go to Temple for Friday

night service before she went out on a date. With all his children, Aaron stressed the religious teaching of their faith, to wit: "to make the world a better place."

Every Sunday evening with the cook off duty, Aaron prepared the same supper for his family—grilled cheese sandwiches and grape juice. The family loved to listen to "Our Miss Brooks" on the radio. When the Gillette Cavalcade of Sports came on, the children knew it was time for bed.

Every school-day morning, Aaron made sure the children were dressed and ready for school while Janet Ann slept late. As they left the house, she called to them from her bed, "Make sure you wear your coat (or take your umbrella), it's cold outside (or it's going to rain)."

The children looked up at their father in wonder. How did she know what the weather was without even poking her head outside? As each of the children reached the age to attend nearby Wynnton School, Aaron walked each one to school every morning. On special occasions, he bought them breakfast at the Krystal—a hamburger, coke, and slice of chocolate cream pie.

"Don't tell your mother," Aaron said as he munched his burger.

After walking the child to school, Aaron took the bus or hitched a ride into town, leaving the family car, a beat up Plymouth station wagon they called the "Gray Goose" for Janet Ann. Walking up Wynnton Road toward town, Aaron prayed he'd catch a ride before he got to Cedar Avenue where an elderly lady named "Aunt Sadie" held court on her porch. When Sadie saw him coming, she'd glance at her watch and call to him, "You're just now going to work? My children left for downtown hours ago."

What she did not realize was that with his law practice still in its infancy, Aaron had no clients waiting for him when he did arrive. Ahead of him stretched long hours of waiting.

On weekends the Cohns filled the station wagon with as many other children as they could fit and drove all over the state to watch Leslie play football, baseball, and basketball. The

Cohns spent their vacation each summer at Eleanor Village near Daytona. Driving down in the Gray Goose with the children's nurse, Essie Mae, they left well before daylight to avoid the heat of the day, armed with boxes of fried chicken and potato salad for a picnic along the way.

As a hot wind blasted through the open windows, Aaron led a family sing-along. He taught the children all the army and University of Georgia fight songs he knew. (Leslie knew the words to "Glory, Glory to Old Georgia" long before he learned the national anthem.) And Janet Ann kept score while the children played games. When they stopped for gas, they sent Jane in to inspect the ladies' restroom for cleanliness.

Finally they arrived at the seashore where the family played in the surf. Every year Aaron was amazed that with all those miles and miles of sand, Gail and Leslie fought over the same piece of it.

At the end of their vacation, Aaron Cohn was happier to see the Columbus city limits sign than he had been to leave it. No matter how much fun they had, for Aaron, there truly was no place like home. Even the water tasted better in Columbus than anywhere else on Earth.

Quiet Etta Cohn came for dinner once a week. Leslie once asked her, "Why do you talk so little?"

Etta replied with a light in her eyes, "You can learn more by listening."

Until her death in 1985, Etta never said an unkind word about anyone, and she made excuses for people who slighted her. The only time she ever felt righteous was over the fate of Julius and Ethel Rosenberg, who were executed in 1953 for passing national secrets to the Soviets on how to make an atomic bomb.

"How could they treat this country this way?" she fretted. When the couple was electrocuted, her family was shocked to hear her say, "They deserve their punishment!"

Like Etta, Aaron normally had a sweet nature. When someone acted petulant, he didn't take it personally. He merely assumed they were having a bad day, so he treated them especially nice. He also was funny, with a dry and quick sense of humor. He loved people, and they returned his affections.

So that Leslie would learn how to respect all kinds of people, Aaron sent him to a YMCA camp. When Leslie returned, he insisted the family say a blessing before their meals just as they had done at camp. Aaron and Janet Ann said, "Fine." So Leslie bowed his head. His parents and sisters bowed theirs too. Then Leslie repeated the prayer he had learned: "Bless this food to the nourishment of our bodies. In Christ's name we pray. Amen."

"Amen," said the others without further comment. Leslie blessed family dinners in this way for months, but as he began attending Hebrew school in preparation for his Bar Mitzvah, his ritual faded away naturally without his parents ever mentioning that his was not the prayer of the Jewish faith.

Perhaps the fact that the family celebrated Chanukah *and* enjoyed a Christmas tree every year had something to do with Leslie's openness to Christianity. Even the devoutly religious Etta Cohn loved the Cohn's Christmas tree, which Janet Ann decorated every year until Gail became a teenager. Then one winter Gail said to her parents, "Don't you think we can do without this now?"

In spite of their openness to Christianity, the Cohn children faced the same prejudice that Aaron had encountered growing up. When Leslie came home from school one day and told his father that he was worried he was going to hell for being Jewish, Aaron asked him: "Do you think Big Mama is going to Heaven?"

"Oh yes," said the boy. Everyone knew his grandmother Etta was a saint.

"And what is she?" asked Aaron.

"She's Jewish."

"Does that answer your question?"

It sure did.

Of course, sports continued to be an integral part of Aaron's life. On Saturdays, Aaron took Leslie with him to the courts at Lake Bottom Park to hit some balls. Leslie soon got bored, but it was usually at this time that someone called over to Aaron

Aaron and the "old men" of the Columbus YMCA volleyball team won ten state championships in a row and placed fifth in the national seniors championship in Memphis in 1957.

saying they needed another player to have a foursome. That's when Leslie hit the jackpot. His father handed him some change and told him to go buy a snow cone. For the next hour, Leslie ate junk food and played on his own.

From the late 1940s through the 1950s Aaron played volleyball every weekend for the Columbus YMCA. Between practicing three times a week and driving to weekend competitions, the sport consumed a lot of his spare time, but Aaron loved the camaraderie. The team paid for their own gas and slept in rooms provided by the host YMCA. Aaron and his roommate, B. F. Young, usually found nothing in their room but two cots and a Gideon Bible. They could not have been happier.

When they faced off against Florida State University one

year, the Floridians took one look at what seemed to them to be old men and assumed they had this game in the bag. But the Columbus men had experience on their side. They beat FSU, and additionally, Aaron's team won ten state volleyball championships in a row. They placed fifth in the national seniors championship in Memphis in 1957.

In addition to the hours of fun he had as an athlete, Aaron enjoyed coaching. For more than ten years, Aaron coached baseball for Leslie's age group, continuing even a couple of years beyond his son's career. To Cohn, the sport itself was fun, but he also saw how he could make a difference in the lives of the children (and their parents) by being a role model of good citizenship. He always was telling the other adults, "Listen, you've got to be fair with these kids because next thing you know you'll turn around and they're gonna be running your city."

Leslie pitched for his Little League team. One day the opposing team was batting with two outs when the third basemen fumbled a line drive, allowing the batter to drive in the winning run and causing Leslie to lose the game.

Afterward Leslie cried in frustration, "I'll never play again!"

Aaron calmly told him, "If you want to be a quitter, fine! It's your decision." End of conversation. The next day Leslie resumed his place on the pitcher's mound, having decided on his own to persevere.

For many years Aaron served on the physical council for the YMCA. He presided over the Parentback Club of Columbus High School and was president of the Columbus Tennis Patrons Association. He, with three others, ran a series of tennis clinics at Lake Bottom Park and the YMCA, hoping to attract black youth into what was then a "white sport" but with limited success.

When Aaron's dear friend Jim Pyburn, the athletic director at Columbus High School, needed help coaching the tennis team, Aaron was glad to pitch in there as well. In one early match a boy continually threw his racket in anger. The coach was about to walk out on the court and eject him when Aaron stopped him.

"Wait for the next court change," he advised, "then mention that if he throws his racket one more time, he'll never play for CHS again." The strategy worked perfectly.

Aaron coached for Peach Little League baseball and occasionally for Pop Warner Football, serving on the latter's board. He loved working with the children and playing a part in molding his son Leslie into a good sport as well as a good athlete. Leslie was tall like his maternal grandfather, and Aaron remarked many times that he wished he had his son's height.

While his girls were not disposed or encouraged to become athletes like Leslie, Aaron did share with them the thrill of watching sports. Gail was about ten years old when she accompanied her father to her first Georgia-Auburn football game at Columbus's Memorial Stadium. For many years thereafter Gail believed everyone yelled "Go dogs!" at the conclusion of the National Anthem.

In 1953 Aaron bought his first pair of season tickets for the University of Georgia football season. Each Friday before a home game he and Janet Ann and their children (and, later, their grandchildren) drove to Athens with the Roddenberys for a fun-filled weekend. Being superstitious, Aaron kept these same seats on the last row of the stadium even after he could afford better ones. He preferred not having unruly people sitting behind him, and the roof that was eventually erected overhead made it more comfortable in any weather.

In 1957 Aaron became president of the local bar association, then known as the Columbus Lawyers Club. Never having had a single misunderstanding with another attorney, he was perfect for the position. The legal profession functioned like a fraternity in the 1950s. It was known for being fair, not flamboyant. Every member knew everyone else, and not only were they all on a first-name basis, but they also knew each other's "people"—their uncles and cousins and where their brothers had gone to school. The standard for excellence among them was set pretty high. One didn't wait for his opposition to lose a case; he worked to win on the merit of his own.

Members of the Columbus Bar liked to joke among themselves that they had had a good month when they "made a couple of fees of five dollars . . . and a couple of small ones too." While hyperbole, this summed up Aaron's early business income fairly well. He and Andy Roddenbery, a medical doctor, often said to one another, "If only we could make ten thousand dollars one year, we'd be happy for the rest of our lives."

All of Aaron's hard work as an attorney began to pay off as one satisfied legal client led to another. By the late 1950s, the Cohns were prospering, as was Temple Israel, which considered constructing a large, new building. At a meeting to discuss this, an old man of the congregation turned to Aaron and said, "You young whippersnappers! How do you think you can afford to pay for a new building?" But Aaron and the other young and upwardly mobile members signed a pledge, committing to a certain level of support for the grand, new building on Wildwood Avenue.

At about this same time, Aaron told his children to pile into the car because he and Janet Ann had something to show them. They stopped at a lovely, sloping lot on Preston Drive in a new neighborhood situated near a new shopping center, the high school, and the new temple. The children noticed how happy their father was about the prospect of building a new house. Aaron tried to explain to them how he would be paying for this house for the next thirty years.

Ten-year-old Leslie asked, "Why do people take so long to pay for a house?"

And Aaron answered, "So they don't have to move for thirty years."

The Cohns hired an architect to design a gracious split-level home for their family of five—six counting the family dog, Rufus. Just when everything seemed to be going well, the telephone jangled to life late one night. A caller told Aaron the First National Bank building was on fire.

Aaron rushed uptown in time to see flames lapping out of the window of his second-floor office, which he shared with his cousin, Aaron Satlof. Inside, many precious keepsakes melted or burned to ash, including the silk military maps he'd brought home from Europe and his most precious tennis trophies. Their law books smoldered. To make matters worse, Aaron had no insurance. His friend Andy Roddenbery told him, "I think the Lord is testing you."

"Well, tell him I don't need it," said Aaron.

But Aaron kept a sense of humor about his travails. "Just think," he kidded his cousin, "All those books were burned before you ever had a chance to read the first one."

With no alternative except to begin again, Cohn set up a partnership with his friend Milton Hirsch in a building next to the YMCA on Eleventh Street. Aaron's clients included refugees from other lands who also were starting over. He never charged any of them. Columbus had given his parents a home in 1906, and he was merely returning the favor. He also represented pro bono the YMCA dormitory and the Valley Rescue Mission, and he met some nice people in the process.

Reeling from the new expenses in simultaneously reestablishing his business, paying his pledge to the temple, and building a new house, the Cohns had to scale down their house plans. Even so, they held fast to their intention to give each child a room of his or her own. In addition to the master suite, there would be two bedrooms upstairs for the girls, and they planned for Leslie to occupy the bedroom in the basement.

The new house on Preston Drive—with a street number that matched Aaron's birth year— soon was complete, but no one except guests ever used the lower bedroom because all of the Cohns preferred to be near each other on the same floor. All through high school Gail shared a room with her baby sister, Jane, so that Leslie could have the other upstairs bedroom.

Aaron's last big surprise for the family was a new stereo system with detachable speakers for the basement. With stereophonic music for dancing replacing their old Victrola, the lowest level of the house became a popular hangout. Under the Cohns' watchful eye the neighborhood children congregated, so the Cohn children had no need of leaving home in order to see their friends.

Both Gail and Jane loved to dance with their father by standing on his feet. "Just relax and let the man lead you," he'd instruct them. And they mastered every dance from the jitterbug to the tango. Even as an adult, Gail said her father was still her favorite dance partner.

When Aaron and Janet Ann dance, people stop what they're doing to watch.

Janet Ann was a lovely dancer also, but she was always generous about sharing Aaron with her girls. Aaron and Janet Ann's favorite song was the Rodgers and Hart ballad "Where or When," and whenever they danced together, people stopped dancing just to watch them. Strains of big band music, Frank Sinatra, and Tony Bennett filled the basement.

Through it all, Aaron's marriage to Janet Ann remained more a love affair than a partnership. Back in 1941 they had meant it when they committed to each other for keeps. When Aaron was not in court or playing ball or going to meetings or making speeches, he and Janet Ann enjoyed the companionship of each other and their extended family. Janet Ann preferred her husband's company to being with most women. He was—and is—her best friend.

Neither of them ever traveled without the other one; however, whenever they attended conferences, Aaron spent as much of his free time playing tennis in pick-up games as possible while Janet Ann sunned by the pool. But in the mid-1960s Aaron and Janet Ann were attending a convention in Jamaica when Aaron said to her over lunch, "Do you see that fat woman over there? Well, if she can play tennis, you can. We're always together except when we go away. I want you to be with me."

So in her forties Janet Ann became Aaron's mixed doubles partner. Together they won a lot of matches and made a lot of friends on the court, in spite of the fact that Aaron took winning seriously. Whenever Janet Ann missed a point, he shook his head and pursed his lips, but he never embarrassed her.

The Cohns seldom entertained for business reasons. When it came to dinner parties, Janet Ann told Aaron, "You are on your own." This suited him just fine. The only people they invited into their home were people they loved and enjoyed. This meant that, following the laws of reciprocity, there were plenty of parties the Cohns were not invited to. But Janet Ann was never sensitive about social slights. As far as she was concerned, her family was her life.

For her and Aaron nothing was more important than supporting their children as they blossomed into young adults. They knew it took more than luck to have good children. The Cohns attended every game, every performance, every PTA meeting.

Disciplining the children was really Aaron and Janet Ann's only bone of contention. Aaron tended to be stricter when the children were young, but in actuality he was the softer one. As they matured Janet Ann was more confrontational while Aaron appealed to their sense of justice. When they misbehaved, he usually asked them, "Do you think what you did was *fair*?" At

The Cohn grandchildren enjoy each other's company.

times Aaron and Janet Ann agreed to disagree. But no matter what argument they may have had, they resolved never to freeze the other one out.

The two of them differed in style. Janet Ann liked the finer things in life. Aaron had not one materialistic bone in his body, and he lived by the maxim that it didn't matter how much money you made; it was how much you held on to that mattered. When the younger children were in high school, Janet Ann drove a new car, but the kids were a bit embarrassed by their father's car, a red Rambler whose front seat collapsed backward when he shifted the gear into reverse. Another of his vehicles, an English Ford, was so hard to crank in the mornings, many a day began with the children and the hired help pushing Aaron's car downhill until the motor fired.

As frugal as Aaron was, he hired a maid and a gardener, and these assistants became part of the family. With a soft spot in his heart for the underdog, Aaron was always there to bail them out—sometimes literally—whenever the employees got themselves in a scrape.

Aaron showed a close affinity for children—all children—

from the outset. He taught his children to set the example for their group of friends, to do the right thing no matter what anyone else did. He instilled in them the belief that doing good works was a privilege. He taught them to get back on the proverbial horse when they got bucked off. He modeled for them that controversy was to be avoided, if possible, but never to back down from a worthy fight.

Gail tagged along with her father during voter registration drives, and she accompanied him when he gave rides to voters. She stuffed March of Dimes letters beside him. She followed him as he spoke to churches and other organizations. She assumed public speaking was not hard because her father did it so effortlessly, so she also became a strong speaker. In other words, Aaron Cohn shaped his children by modeling the values he held dear.

But Cohn also could be strict. When Leslie decided one day that he didn't want to go to Wynnton School any more, Aaron grabbed him in a headlock and plopped him down on his desk.

"I don't want to ever hear you say you don't want to go to school again," he told his son. And that was that.

When Leslie was in high school, he was late for curfew only once. Unfortunately for him, a policeman stopped him for speeding as he hurried home. When Aaron took his son to traffic court, the judge said, "Well, I guess you're here to get your son off."

"On the contrary," said Aaron. "I'm here to make sure he gets what's coming to him."

Sure enough, when the judge formally asked the defendant how he pled, Aaron shouted, "Guilty!"

Looking at his father in shock, Leslie decided on the spot that Aaron Cohn was a terrible lawyer. "I could have done better than that by myself!" he complained.

Gail was sixteen when she suffered the great misfortune to collide with a police car. The policeman tried to ascertain if she was hurt, but all Gail could do was sob, "My father's going to kill me!"

The policeman said, "Calm down. Calm down. Let me see your license."

He looked at it and then back at her.

"Are you Aaron Cohn's daughter?" he asked.

"Yes," she sniffled.

"You're right," he said. "Your father *is* going to kill you."

Actually, when Aaron saw how upset Gail already was, he didn't punish her. Generally his girls were easy to manage. Their curfew was midnight, and if there were still friends hanging around at that hour, Aaron blinked the lights in the basement, and everyone cleared out.

Leslie required a firmer hand. Late one night he was smoking in the downstairs bathroom with the window open when Aaron called down to him from the head of the stairs to ask him what he was doing. Not realizing the wind was blowing his smoke into the hallway behind him, Leslie lied. Aaron asked him twice more if he wanted to change his story; each time Leslie stuck to it. Aaron exploded in rage. He had not a mean bone in his body, but there was one thing he would not tolerate—deception. To him, the truth never could be worse than a lie.

Aaron told his children he would never send them to a private school. "That's not what the world is all about," he said. "You have to learn to get along with everyone." This value he must have taught them well because it extended beyond their generation. Leslie's children decided not to attend a fine private school even though at least one of them was eligible for a scholarship.

Even though Aaron was usually upbeat and positive, he reminded his children occasionally that one day their friends might exclude them. He hoped to prepare them for the day when they tasted their first social prejudice so that they would not be devastated by it. When those hurtful moments came, Cohn reminded his children not to take it personally because that's just how people were.

"Do the right thing, and move forward," he told them.

When Gail grew up, she was excluded from the Junior

League because of her faith. Since she'd been forewarned, she was not devastated. But when the same organization later invited Aaron to speak to them and he accepted, Gail was furious.

"They wouldn't let me join their club, and now you're pandering to them?"

Aaron shrugged. "There has to be a trailblazer sometime," he said. "Prejudice is passed down from one generation to another, but it has to stop at some point." Gail was shocked when her father became the first person of the Jewish faith to serve on the board of the Junior League. Many years later, she admitted her father had been right to try to work from within to repair a broken system.

During the war Aaron had seen the black soldiers of the 761st Tank Battalion put their lives on the line for their country. Back in Columbus after the war, Aaron abhorred the Jim Crow laws that made the African American community de facto second-class citizens. He hoped one day he would be in a position to do his part in bettering race relations in Columbus. His chance came in 1960 when Superior Court Judges A. E. Davis, John H. Land, and J. R. Thompson asked Aaron to become the new Chief Voter Registrar for Muscogee County. Since this offer came at a time when the civil rights movement was picking up steam, overseeing the registration of black voters who never had been allowed to vote before was "a real hot potato." Aaron never had aspired to politics, but he could not turn down his city when it needed him.

He told the judges how strongly he felt that minorities should suffer no discrimination or persecution. They told him they expected nothing less of him than to be fair, so he took the job, which paid twenty dollars a month, netting after taxes and social security deductions $3.62.

As soon as Aaron began, representatives of both the white and black communities started pressuring him to do things their way. J. R. Allen of the Junior Chamber of Commerce was a good friend and future mayor. He wanted Cohn to deputize the Jaycees and use them to register voters in certain areas of town. Meanwhile a CORE (Congress of Racial Equality) leader wanted Cohn to set up voter registration in other areas of town. When Aaron resisted this idea, the man accused Cohn of discriminating. Aaron told the black man it was against his religion to discriminate.

The CORE official threatened to take Aaron's job.

"Do you want my job?" Aaron asked. "Well, let me tell you what it pays."

When Cohn told him what he made for all that aggravation, the guy said, "Man, you're kidding me!"

"No, man!" Aaron assured him. "I'm not kidding you!"

He backed off, and Aaron went ahead and did things his way—the fair way. The city set up circus tents on Broadway between Eleventh and Twelfth Streets, near the bus station so that all would have access. And for the first time in Columbus, Georgia, black workers registered white voters and whites registered blacks. Cohn instructed the volunteers to pass on to him anyone who gave them trouble. To his relief, his colleagues were a fine group of people. The operation ran beautifully, and they registered thousands of new voters. There were no problems and no complaints.

For the five most crucial years of the civil rights movement (1960-65) Aaron continued to supervise voter registration. In other cities, federal voting officials monitored the process to be sure the registration was conducted fairly. There was no need for that in Columbus where the whole affair was old news by the time activists resorted to marching from Selma to Montgomery in protest of unfair voting procedures in Alabama, leading to the Voting Rights Act of 1965, which insured for other municipalities the same rights that Columbus voters had enjoyed for years.

By 1965 it was becoming clear to his community that they were blessed to have Aaron Cohn as a fellow citizen. Cohn served on the board of trustees of the Home Federal Loan Association where he and Forest Champion insisted that any capable lawyer should be added to the list of approved attorneys who could be hired to handle closings. That way the younger attorneys would not have to struggle as Cohn had twenty years earlier. Cohn also sat on the board of Blue Cross and Blue Shield of Georgia (later chairing a part of this organization in 1985).

Aaron also had organized the polio board and the first "Mother's March" for the March of Dimes campaign. He joined the executive board of the Georgia Hospital Association and became the third vice-commander of the local chapter of the Military Order of World Wars. He sat on the local USO executive board and advised the Selective Service System. He joined (and later became president of) the Muscogee Lion's Club, taking daughter Gail with him as he sold brooms door-to-door to raise money for the blind. And without a doubt, Cohn was the city's most spirited member of the local Georgia Bulldog Club.

Aaron also served on the State Crime Commission and on the executive boards of Goodwill Industries, the Chattahoochee Council of the Boy Scouts, Little League Baseball, the Pop Warner Football Program, and the Columbus College Athletic Fund. He also headed the Junior Achievement Program of Columbus. All of these contributions he had made while remaining active in the Army Reserves and rising to the rank of colonel.

Like their father, the Cohn children were rising in their community's regard. Gail and Jane blossomed into fine ladies, active in helping many philanthropic non-profit programs in their respective communities. Three of Aaron's proudest moments associated with son Leslie were when Leslie became a Distinguished Military Graduate of the University of Georgia, when he graduated from law school, and when he became his father's partner in the law firm of Cohn and Cohn in 1973.

Standing midway through a long and remarkable life, Aaron Cohn already had become the embodiment of the words of Hillel, the revered Jewish scholar and sage: "If I am not for myself, who will be for me? But if I am for myself [alone], what am I? And if not now, when?"

CHAPTER 13

ALL RISE!

After Aaron had served as Muscogee County's Chief of Voter Registration for four years, two superior court judges approached him at the end of 1964 about becoming the next juvenile court judge. It was a part-time position but one that tugged at Aaron's heart. Knowing of the sad end of so many beautiful children during the Holocaust, the protection and direction of minors, more than any other field, called to him.

The first juvenile court in the nation had been established in Chicago just a few years before Aaron's parents immigrated to America. Muscogee County created its first juvenile court in the 1920s. Every child under the age of seventeen who committed an offense, "no matter how serious or minor" came before Juvenile Court. Judge Polly Lamar, Aaron's old nemesis (the woman who forbade him to bring his tennis racket into the law library before the war), had been appointed judge of Muscogee County Juvenile Court in 1941. Only one other judge (Stanford Willis) succeeded her by the time Aaron was offered the job.

Janet Ann didn't want Aaron to accept the post on the juvenile court bench because he would occasionally be passing judgment on the children of people they knew well, and there were bound to be misunderstandings. But Aaron pointed out what a positive difference he could make in children's lives. After

Col. Aaron Cohn retired from the Army Reserves in 1965 to become judge of the Juvenile Court of Muscogee County.

Janet Ann pled her case for hours one night, Aaron finally told her he wouldn't take the job.

"Go to bed and quit badgering me," he pleaded.

But after sleeping on it, Cohn saw things differently in the morning. He told Janet Ann he was going downtown to take that job, after all. On December 30, 1964, Superior Court Judge J. Alvan Davis swore Aaron in, and he became the first Jewish judge in Columbus history. When Charlie Goodrum, a middle school principal on the south side of town heard the news, he was elated. "We got us a horse now, and we're really gonna ride him."

Aaron took office just as a rise in juvenile crime, teenage pregnancy, and pornography swept the nation. Like no previous generation, the youth of the 1960s disrespected such perennial symbols of authority as parents and policemen. The newly minted judge told civic groups the country needed to return to the Fourth Commandment to "honor thy father and thy mother." He told youth, "It doesn't take guts to steal a car or break the law. It takes guts to do the right thing."

Cohn explained the nature of his court to the local newspaper, "This is not a criminal court in the sense of punishment, but it is designed toward rehabilitation . . . [of] children from all economic levels and racial backgrounds . . ." Cohn said he could relate well to the very young on certain matters because as he put it, "I was a naughty little boy. Thank goodness I learned that it just didn't pay to stay naughty."

Besides his own transgressions, Cohn also could relate

to delinquents because in the 1920s some of his friends and neighbors on Fourth Avenue had been a rough and tumble lot. When a couple of his high school acquaintances had gone to jail, they were locked up with adult felons because there had been no separate facility for youth.

The home town newspaper reported that the new judge believed that "children need love first, along with a sense of discipline." Once they were assured that support, they would come to respect their parents. And once respect was established, "the other vital forms needed to mold character become accepted easily."

Burglary was the most prevalent type of case brought before his court in the 1960s. This crime even hit the judge's office when someone stole money from the court's petty cash box. But after Cohn had worked for a little over a year, a Muscogee County Grand Jury's juvenile committee noted a downward trend in the number of juvenile cases coming before Judge Cohn's court. They reported that the reason for this trend seemed to be that "juveniles now understand that they will be punished for their wrongdoings."

The grand jury committee reported that it was Aaron Cohn's philosophy "not to pamper [children] . . . but to let them know they are responsible for their actions and will be punished for their transgressions."

Even though the community was impressed with the new judge's get-tough attitude, there remained ample reason for the juvenile court to be classified as an "Inferior Court" since it lay at the lowest rung of power and prestige within the court system. Aaron's courtroom was, in his opinion, "in the worst possible place it could be," occupying a small, dark, and gloomy room next to the janitor's closet in the basement of the courthouse where probation officers crowded into little stalls. The cramped room spoke volumes about how little society valued children.

In his tiny courtroom the new judge heard many heart-breaking stories of neglect and abuse by parents, who were hardly more than children themselves. He noted the clean but threadbare clothes that many defendants donned for their day in court, and yet there was so little he could do about the poverty, unemployment, bigotry, and health issues that were turning these children into outlaws. By the time Cohn encountered a delinquent child in his courtroom, his life was already in crisis.

Cohn's decisions addressed what was best for the child's future while at the same time protecting the public. Grappling with the often-opposing vantage points of parents, victims, and the press made matters more complicated. "Monday morning quarterbacks" abounded. Yet for all the challenges he faced, he earned only $7,800.

The judge's goal generally was to be "fair, firm, and friendly," but he could scare the living daylights out of kids with a scowl that was reminiscent of "the Great and Powerful Oz." With eyes flashing in anger, Judge Cohn could slap his desk so hard it seemed the earth shook and thunder rolled. The judge moved surprisingly fast to judgment, and when people looked surprised by that, he told them, "I was in the US Cavalry, son. We moved fast."

Cohn often explained his decisions by saying, "I will not use a 150 mm. gun to shoot a sparrow, nor will I use a pop gun to slay an elephant." Sometimes he was loving and empathetic (the pop gun). Sometimes he was wrathful like the cannon. In his brief encounter with each child he intuited what each needed to turn his life around. He seemed to know instantly which child needed to be scared to tears and which needed to be assured that someone in this big, mean world loved him.

Though justice was swift, coworkers noticed that not one single time did he make the wrong decision. "It's a gift to be able to look at a child and know how to treat each one for maximum effect," said courtroom coordinator Carolyn Hester. Sometimes his tactic was reproach, telling the kid, "You're an ungrateful, spoiled child. You ought to hug and kiss your mother every day. Where's your father? See? What would you do without her?" He told many a young person, "You don't know how lucky you are to be an American."

Judge Aaron Cohn sits in chambers.

Then just as readily, Cohn offered the carrot instead of the stick. He told some children how much he cared about them. He hoped they would grow up to be good citizens and have good lives, and he offered them leniency and inspiration. He gave them the gift of accountability, telling them he would keep tabs on them, and he expected them to stay in school, accomplish great things, and become model citizens.

He told angry, defensive parents, "I care about your family. I care about your son too. But I want him to be a son you can be proud of." Those who witnessed Cohn in action were stunned by his effectiveness. His secretary, Frances King, said, "When he tells it like it is in that courtroom, I get goose bumps. He's a forceful man."

Although his job could be demanding and even frustrating,

Aaron could not have been more passionate about it. Later as he looked back on his career he said, "If I had not become a juvenile court judge I would have been just another lawyer." But as a juvenile judge he was able to touch the lives of poor children—the true underdogs of society—and turn many of them to the light. And because of Judge Aaron Cohn, hundreds, if not thousands, of children avoided a revolving life of crime and incarceration leading down a dead end street.

Cohn knew he was not in court to win a popularity contest. The army had taught him that making unpopular decisions was just a part of being a good leader. Aaron's only criterion was to make a decision that protected the public but gave the child every chance to reform. So long as Aaron felt he'd done the right thing for each child, he was happy, even when others might find fault with his decision. He never held a grudge against those angered by his decisions. In his mind, they had a right to be vexed, but when he accepted the post of juvenile judge he was sworn to answer to a higher authority. In what turned out to be a very long career on the bench, Judge Cohn never experienced the burnout others in his position experienced because he was not burdened with the stress of second-guessing his decisions.

Ironically, by not trying to win a popularity contest, he actually won the heart of his city. Columbus Mayor Butch Martin said publicly that "Of all the lawyers and judges [he knew] in Columbus, Judge Cohn is the most well-liked and most respected. He earned this respect because he has always been honest and upright."

Inside and outside of the courtroom, Cohn became children's most powerful advocate. Refusing no invitation to speak on their behalf, he made the rounds at virtually every community meeting. He told the PTA, "There is no more difficult job than raising good children." He told the YMCA, "Children must know, obey, and respect the teachings of God." He told the Kiwanis Club, "We cannot expect to turn our children over to the public schools [or] to Sunday school, . . . and have them raise them for us." He reminded other civic groups, "What happens to this country depends on what kind of children we raise." He told others, "There is no doubt about it. The more boy scouts we can have, the less juvenile delinquency there will be."

When two teenagers found three hundred dollars in the street and turned it over to police, the judge sent them letters of praise. "Contrary to what others may think," he wrote, "honesty is still the first requisite of good character."

At the time when Cohn became a judge in 1965, the juvenile court system treated children tyrannically. Neither police nor witnesses were required to testify against the accused. There were no court-appointed lawyers to defend the children, who had no rights to cross-examine witnesses or appeal decisions.

But the times were changing. Soon after taking office, Cohn attended a national seminar in 1966 where he heard Omar Ketchum (the former president of the National Council of Juvenile and Family Court Judges) say that children should be entitled to a lawyer under the Fourteenth Amendment. Cohn was convinced, and he came home and told Superior Court Judge John Land that they were going to need lawyers to represent the children. Land told him there was no money to pay legal fees, so Cohn appealed to a dozen local attorneys whom he knew well from his extra-curricular activities playing tennis and coaching baseball. He asked them if they would represent a child as defense council if needed, and all vowed to pitch in.

After this practice was already in place in Columbus, the US Supreme Court ruled in 1967 in the landmark Gault Decision that under the Fourteenth Amendment, juveniles should have the same rights as adults. Soon thereafter, the nation instituted rules for fairness to children. Juveniles had to be given adequate notice of their charges, the right to counsel, the right to cross-examination of sworn witnesses, and the privilege against self-incrimination.

Since Judge Cohn already had instituted many of these protections and procedures, the Columbus newspaper applauded Cohn's "forward-looking, progressive nature." But as far as the judge was concerned, this was no time to rest on his laurels. There being no jury in juvenile cases, the judge, in addition to being the traditional father figure to the delinquent, also had to stay abreast of all the "due process" requirements of the Constitution as the Supreme Court interpreted them, and these standards were changing swiftly with the times.

The judge explained the dilemma he faced when he wrote an article for the *Georgia Bar Journal.* "The judge . . . must be sensitive to the needs of the youngsters while considering the welfare and security of the community. He must listen to his critics in search of better avenues of approach to the problems he faces, but he must stand steadfast with his own principles when hard decisions must be made. And finally, he must be always conscious of the constitutional rights of those before him because he knows that any judgment, however sound in concept and potential effect, could be void if procedural safeguards are not observed. In short, he must act in the knowledge that the future of the youngster involved as well as any appellate court reversal based on his court proceedings truly depends upon his knowledge, legal ability, wisdom, and sense of fair play . . . We must continually study and strive to meet the challenges and goals of juvenile justice. Certainly, we can do no less for the children of Georgia."

Realizing the weight of responsibility Cohn shouldered, one of the Superior Court judges asked how he could help lessen his burden. Aaron told him his first priority was in finding better quarters for his courtroom. Although the judge wanted to help Aaron, there seemed to be nowhere to accommodate the juvenile court. The county government long ago had outgrown its building, occupying every corner of space both in the courthouse and in its annex, Foley House, across the street.

But when a fire destroyed Foley House, the county no longer had the liberty of ignoring its critical need for more space. Superior Court judges asked Aaron if he knew of any house near the courthouse that could be rented for the juvenile court so that county law enforcement could claim his rooms in the courthouse basement. Aaron said yes, as a matter of fact, he knew an ideal building.

His childhood home right across the street was then lying vacant after Etta Cohn had moved out of her home at 831 Second Avenue for a smaller retirement home. So when his mother rented her house out to become Aaron's juvenile court, Aaron's life came full circle.

With very little renovation, Aaron converted the Cohn family's former music room, where Aaron had practiced the trumpet, into the new courtroom. The old benches lining the walls made excellent spectator seating. Aaron transformed the old kitchen into his chambers. In comparison to the courthouse basement, this old house provided a spacious and airy ambience that felt less punitive and more caring.

There was no security to speak of in the new facility. The doors were never locked during office hours. A delinquent ran out of the courtroom one day and down Second Avenue, making it to Eleventh Street before probation officer and former UGA track star Homer DeLoach caught up with him. (After that incident, Cohn joked that henceforth the job requirements for all new probation officers should include experience on a track team.)

The court also had no set hours. Cohn merely held court whenever a case needed hearing. Two referees handled traffic matters, and Aaron heard all cases that could lead to incarceration. He continued to practice law on the side to earn a good living, but the juvenile court always remained his highest priority.

Although the juvenile court position was considered part-time, Aaron's day usually began at 7:30, and it didn't end when he left his office. Sometimes he had a restless night, pondering a decision he'd make on the morrow. His home telephone rang at all hours. Janet Ann pled with Aaron to get a private line, but he said, "I am a servant of the people, and their problems don't stop with the setting of the sun."

Aaron's most onerous duty as juvenile court judge was administering the run-down youth detention center on Schatulga Road. It seemed to Cohn a conflict of interest to be simultaneously judge and administrator of the correctional institution. He told the county commission he was a judge, not a jailer. Why couldn't his court create a position analogous to the sheriff who served the superior court? But money was tight, and he was told there simply was no one else to do it but he.

Aaron often slept fitfully, worried about the children locked inside the neglected facility. If a fire had started in the middle of the night, who would save them? He investigated what was needed to renovate the old building and learned he would need seventeen thousand dollars. He made an appointment with a county official to plead his case, but the clerk told him the bridge over Uchee Creek needed repairs, and that was more important than troubled children.

Without the funds for upkeep of the home, Aaron felt his job was only half done. He continued to plead his case to anyone who would listen. Finally in 1971 with consolidation of the city and county governments, the youth facility was placed under the supervision of the Public Safety Director, Joe Sargis, and together Cohn and Sargis began lobbying for a new detention home.

They asked legislator Floyd Hudgins to sponsor a bill to appropriate the money for it, and when Hudgins was successful the resultant new building (also on Schatulga Road) had more security than before and was twice as large. At last Judge Cohn could rest easily, knowing the children were safe in detention.

The facility looked like a "longish brick building," not too different from a home except there were bars on the windows. The delinquents lived in cells and were locked in at night, but during the day they attended classes and played sports in the back lot. A small room without light (known as the "dark room") contained nothing but a coverless toilet. Each newcomer spent fifteen minutes in this space, just to learn it was there. The experience was said to have a settling effect on angry newcomers. The new facility housed twice as many youth as the previous one had, and with the safety of the children assured, Cohn could focus again on the administration of his courtroom and the improvement of juvenile court statewide.

As he went about the state for meetings, Aaron noted that

most of his peers carried an unspoken prejudice against working as a juvenile court judge. Most saw it merely as a stepping stone on the way to presiding over more prestigious courts. But for Aaron, there was never a greater calling than working with and for the children.

In 1971, the same year that the new youth detention center opened, Gail Cohn learned the Sertoma Club was seeking nominations for its "Service to Mankind Award." In Gail's mind no one was more deserving than her father. She carefully composed her nomination and mailed it. In December the announcement came. Aaron Cohn had won the award.

"I'm not sure which of us is most proud, Dad or me," Gail said. She also was thrilled to get to introduce Aaron as the award recipient. At the banquet Gail finally had an opportunity to honor her father, who had given so much to others. And Aaron was impressed by her speaking ability. Apparently she was a chip off the old block.

Since returning from the war Aaron had given much to his community and, although he expected nothing in return, had received little in the way of formal recognition for his efforts. Until the Sertoma award came in December 1971, Aaron had received only one award from his community—the Lion's Club Man of the Year. The Sertoma award, made all the sweeter because his daughter was responsible for his receiving it, turned a corner in the measure of how his community acknowledged his service.

After ten years on the bench, Aaron possessed the clout to promote court employees who had been overlooked by society until then. In 1975 Judge Cohn announced promotions for juvenile court personnel, reflecting his progressive regard for minorities. One of the promotions went to a black man who, because of Cohn, became "probably the only black chief probation officer in the South," declared the local paper. At the same time Aaron gave a Columbus woman the chance to become perhaps the first female in Georgia to serve as a senior probations officer.

Although Aaron was nearing sixty years old in an era

Judge Cohn hams it up for a *Columbus Ledger-Enquirer* photographer. Cohn was known to wear tennis togs under his robes so he could rush to his matches after work.

when thirty was considered "over the hill," he still loved fierce athletic competition. Wearing tennis togs under his judge's robes, he dashed out to Cooper Creek Park after work every Monday, Wednesday, and Friday afternoon to play with his regular foursome (Terry Scott, Fred Kirby, Andy Sheils, and himself). Cohn had served on the board of directors that had created the park in 1972, and there he played many matches and tournaments. It always thrilled him to come to the park and see its thirty courts full of players having the time of their lives. When he had begun playing tennis, he was one of only a handful who cared about the sport.

On the tennis court Aaron earned a different kind of respect. Teammates and opponents alike called the judge "fearless," and partners endured a memorably icy glare when they made a strategic error. Everyone knew how much Aaron Cohn hated to lose. But with a twinkle in his eye, he reminded them there was nothing wrong with being competitive, so long as one was also fair.

In the early 1970s big name tennis pros came to Columbus to compete in the Royal Crown Tennis Classic and the Virginia Slims (Ladies) Tournament at the Columbus Country Club. Cohn usually had the prime seat for these matches because he sat in the umpire's chair, passing judgment on the shots of professionals of the caliber of Wimbledon winners Ken Rosewall and Billie Jean King.

Aaron Cohn and Terry Scott won the 1976 state senior doubles championship.

Before every match while the pros were warming up, Cohn introduced the gallery to each player, announcing their backgrounds "to set the stage." And when they were ready to begin play, Cohn fired off, "Ready on the right? Ready on the left? Play!"

Cohn was loud and clear in his directives and, of course, consummately fair as an umpire. Billie Jean King liked him so much that she asked the judge to call all her matches. There was even talk that Cohn should consider judging at the US Open, but Aaron was content to serve at the occasional tournament in his home town, the greatest city on Earth as far as he was concerned. And besides, he was much too busy playing tennis himself. In the nation's bicentennial year Aaron and Terry Scott won the Georgia Closed Seniors Tournament.

So as not to have a conflict of interest with his work as a judge, Cohn handled no criminal cases in his law practice. He accepted corporate work such as titles and estates—the kinds of cases that did not require one to appear in court. His law office, which he shared with Emmet Cartledge, was located conveniently in a new building across the street from the YMCA. It was there in 1971 that he hired Frances King, sight unseen, over the telephone to become his secretary—without ever checking a reference or shaking her hand.

During Frances's first days in the office, Aaron intimidated her without meaning to. He came in every morning and kissed her on the cheek, but otherwise retained a formal, professional demeanor. She had worked for him for several months before she ever heard him laugh. Each week as she neared completion of a new set of real estate transaction documents, Aaron wore the carpet thin pacing in front of her desk. For him, being late for a closing was out of the question. Perhaps it was his military training that caused him to think that everything he did must be completed ahead of schedule.

Once the ice was broken between Frances and her boss, she began to see the judge's gentler side. "It was a warm place to work," she says now, presently in her thirty-seventh year of employment. According to the current courtroom coordinator, Carolyn Hester, after all that time Frances became the judge's "right hand, his left hand, and his right foot."

Aaron looked forward to the day when he would practice law with his son Leslie who graduated from Samford University Law School and then served in the US Army as a military policeman. Aaron told Leslie that when the time came, he did not expect his son to be the smartest lawyer in Columbus, but he did want him to have the most integrity. "If you're conscientious and fair, you'll make a living," he promised him.

In 1972 as Columbus City government became the first metropolis in Georgia to merge its government with the county, the new fourteen-story tower of the Muscogee County Courthouse became the city's only skyscraper, and the associated three-story wings on either side provided plenty of room for the juvenile court to join the other courtrooms and offices. Aaron's court vacated his parents' home then, but Aaron retained the Second Avenue building as his law office. While he had waited on Leslie to join him in practice in 1973, Aaron had shared offices with Frank "Butch" Martin for eight years. The two of them had only grown closer during the years they worked side by side.

Butch called Aaron "El Magnifico," a moniker coined by Aaron's daughter Gail because whenever Aaron returned from one of his engagements in his endless rounds of speechmaking on the "PTA Circuit," Gail always inquired how it went, and Aaron usually winked and said, "I was magnificent."

The judge's speechmaking circuit widened to include the entire state in 1972 when Aaron became president of the Georgia Juvenile Court Judges Association. This position gave him an even higher bully pulpit for child advocacy. At that time Columbus's state legislator, Floyd Hudgins, worked to push through legislation that prevented a juvenile "status offender" (one who has committed no crime but is a behavior problem to society) from being thrown in the common jails with hard-core criminals. Cohn was the only juvenile court judge in the state who worked actively for the passage of the bill, but his reputation "was a deciding factor in getting the legislation passed," said Hudgins.

The new Hudgins legislation required the state to provide other places to house the delinquents, including foster homes, group homes, and detention homes. Cohn then recruited citizens who would offer their homes as foster homes, appealing to the local ministerial association, among other organizations. Next Judge Cohn fathered a plan employing a volunteer panel of citizens to review the cases of families whose children had been placed in foster homes to determine if the parents were taking the corrective actions the court had prescribed.

In 1975 Gov. George Busbee appointed Aaron to the Governor's Commission on Court Organization and Structure. Cohn also began to guest lecture for Columbus College's Criminal Justice Department and at the Georgia Police Academy in Atlanta.

When Aaron attended an Atlanta meeting of the National Council of Juvenile Court Judges with Janet Ann, both of them were impressed by the quality of people in this organization. The juvenile judges they met acted with no motive of personal power and prestige. This was a diverse group of jurists representing the left and the right but with one prime motivation in common, the children of America. Cohn became active in the organization and soon was elected to their board of trustees.

The more involved he became, the more he enjoyed it. Before long Aaron became a member of the board of the National Council of Juvenile and Family Court Judges, then secretary, vice-president, and finally president of this venerable judicial organization in 1982–83. As president, he acted as "the nation's spokesman for juvenile justice," traveling all over the country to address a myriad of powerful people—policy makers, lawyers, and judges— on issues related to juvenile and family court.

His home town newspaper began to take note of his influence. "Mention Columbus to any of thousands of professionals across the country associated with juvenile justice," it crowed, "and there will be a warm and positive reaction. They know it is the home of their leader, Aaron Cohn. They also know that because of Judge Cohn . . . Columbus has an outstanding juvenile justice system."

Leslie, Jane, Janet Ann, and Gail were present in Portland, Oregon when Aaron was inducted as president of the National Council of Juvenile and Family Court Judges in 1982.

In spite of all his professional activities, Aaron's primary focus remained the children. The most heart-wrenching decisions he made had to do with deprivation cases in which he had to consider taking a child away from his parents. In the termination of parental rights Aaron agreed with the chief justice of the Michigan Supreme Court who termed it "the nearest judgeship in the world to playing God." As Aaron paraphrased her, "God gives parents a child and I'm the only judge, basically, that can take that child away . . . And nobody wants to play God."

Additionally issues of child custody related to divorce cases were added to his "part-time" docket in the 1970s. These cases took much more time to prepare, adding so many hours to his workweek that his private practice had to be slashed, and Aaron dropped out of membership in the Lion's Club.

But he took his expanding powers seriously, keeping his

prime focus on the children. He told a reporter, "We're a people's court because we don't deal in money, we deal with families—the American family." He told another reporter, "I don't care if the children are white or black, rich or poor or whether they have influence or they don't . . . We want to treat all the children fairly. It's very important that the court get a reputation of being a fair court. I can't please everybody. I don't intend to please everybody. But I will be fair."

Another journalist asked him about the growing problems America faced regarding discipline in the public schools. "We (judges) have become so engrossed with individual children's rights that we have undercut school administrators . . . American courts have stripped the schools of parental authority and they've become mere custodians of the children rather than being able to discipline the children. And I think this is one of the reasons schools throughout the country are having such a problem because there is that lack of discipline. I think basically what it amounts to is that children want to be disciplined—fairly and firmly. And I'm not so sure that you could argue that they're rebelling against a lack of proper adult intervention."

So many journalists and community members were asking the judge's advice on the rearing and caring of children that it was clear his city was coming to think of him as a patriarch. Although he would have liked to have worked full-time as a juvenile judge, Cohn still had to practice law in order to make ends meet. After Butch Martin moved on from Cohn's Second Avenue office to become city mayor, a succession of other young attorneys rented offices from Cohn, finding the rent cheap, the location across from the courthouse ideal, and the company inspiring. Fellow members of the bar began referring to Aaron as "the Godfather," but Butch Martin and Aaron's dear friend, Paul Kirkpatrick, joked that he was more a "slum lord."

When Leslie Cohn joined his father's law practice in 1973, this milestone was a dream-come-true for Aaron. For the next twenty-seven years, father and son practiced together on Second Avenue, although they worked in separate spheres of law. Each

Aaron's former home on Second Avenue became the juvenile court, then his law office.

one considered the other to be the "senior partner," and yet both quietly acknowledged that Frances King was really the boss.

Cohn enjoyed mentoring the younger generation, but he did not consider himself too old to be perfected as a jurist. In 1983 he began taking some international credits in juvenile justice at the University of Edinburgh, followed by other courses at international conferences in Amsterdam, The Netherlands, and in Turin, Italy, in 1990. He also began to serve his alma mater as a member of the Board of Visitors of the University of Georgia Law School from 1984 to 1987.

Aaron and his mother remained very close until her death in 1985, and he was equally kind to his mother-in-law, by then a widow. In 1977 Aaron's brother Sol died of a brain tumor. Etta wanted to see Sol one last time, so Aaron and Leslie accompanied her to the funeral home. Etta looked anxious as she looked at her son in his casket. When Aaron asked her what was wrong, she said she wanted to kiss Sol goodbye, but she was too short to reach him.

"Don't worry, Mama," Aaron said, "I'll kiss him goodbye for you."

Aaron remained his mother's rock and his oldest daughter's anchor, her reality check. Gail counted on him to tell her the truth as he saw it. When she returned home to live with her parents after a devastating divorce, she collapsed in the safety of their loving arms. But after she'd spent a few weeks licking her wounds, Aaron walked into her bedroom one day and said, "I didn't raise any weak children. Get up out of that bed, and take care of your children!" So, she did.

But just for good measure, while Gail and her boys were still under his roof, Aaron took her sons, Howie and David, down to tour the youth detention center. He purposely showed them the holding cell.

"See this, boys?" he asked. "Well, this is the last time you will ever see it because if you ever do drugs, I'll kill you myself."

On another day, Aaron pressed young Howie to obey him.

"I'm the boss," Aaron reminded the boy.

"No! You're the judge." Howie replied. "*I'm* the boss."

For several years Aaron was David and Howie's only father figure, but other grandchildren also felt a close connection with their "Poppy." Only occasionally did the children realize the judge was also human. When Leslie's son Al was six years old, Leslie began teaching the youngster how to be a good sport. Al stretched his mind to understand the concept as teaching moments presented themselves over several days.

"Doing your best is more important than winning or losing," Leslie explained one day as he pushed Al in a swing at Lake Bottom Park.

Nearby Aaron was playing a tennis match with Terry Scott, and every so often, a curse word popped out of Aaron's mouth and drifted over to them. Leslie decided it best to walk Al home.

Along the way Al said to his father, "Dad, I know what a good sport is."

"What?" asked Leslie, pleased that his lessons finally had landed.

"Not Poppy," said Al.

In 1983 at the age of sixty-seven Aaron was playing tennis with Bob Flournoy when he began to notice what felt like a lump in his neck. He called his best friend and physician Andy Roddenbery who connected him with a cardiologist. Doctors told Aaron he needed an operation—a quintuple bypass surgery and a pacemaker implant. Before he had time to think, Aaron had checked into the hospital at the University of Alabama, Birmingham. His family was frightened. Aaron Cohn was the glue that held them together. But he told all of them, "Don't worry. This is a piece of cake."

This was a phrase they had heard him use countless times, and since his predictions always came true, they breathed easier. Aaron was nothing if not resilient. After he recovered, he helped his daughter Jane persevere through a cancer scare with this same positive outlook. When he told her, "You'll be okay," and he showed her he clearly was not frightened by the diagnosis, she was able to keep her center.

Aaron resumed playing tennis soon after his heart surgery and continued to play vigorously. But every time he picked up his racket, Janet Ann grew nervous as a cat, fearing he would collapse on the courts. The doctors also warned him to take it easy and stop playing to win.

But how could a man like Aaron Cohn do that? If he was not giving it his all, what was the point of competition? One day when he and a partner were playing against opponents, who had not won a single game in two sets, at triple set point of the second set, Aaron told his partner, "Don't let up. They could still come back."

Whenever Aaron headed for the courts, Janet Ann asked him, "What are you trying to prove?"

"I'm not trying to prove anything," he told her. "I'm just trying to have fun!"

Some days he sneaked out just to avoid a conflict, but

inevitably Janet Ann would be playing at Cooper Creek Park herself that day and catch him in the act.

Finally, in 1996—the year Aaron turned eighty—he conceded to his wife and doctor. After playing tennis and loving every minute of it for more than seventy years, Aaron Cohn put down his racket for good. And it broke his heart. In solidarity with him, Janet Ann quit playing that same day. Then, for exercise, they began walking the "figure eight" at Weracoba Park, but it just wasn't as satisfying.

Aaron is among three honored at a 1992 reunion for their outstanding contributions to the UGA tennis program. Dan Magill (far right) was head tennis coach at this time and Manuel Diaz (far left) was assistant coach but later became head coach. Both Magill and Diaz coached teams to a number of NCA and SEC tennis titles.

Even though the business of being a juvenile court judge consumed him, in many ways Cohn had remained a soldier. After active service in World War II, he had entered the US Army Reserves and had become a colonel, reporting for weekend and summer trainings for nineteen years. In 1957 he became Commander of the Columbus-Fort Benning Chapter of the Military Order of the World Wars.

In 1965, the same year that he accepted the position as juvenile court judge, Aaron had received a letter from the Department of Defense that forced him to choose between two occupational paths, both of which thrilled him. The letter informed him he was in the zone of consideration for promotion to the rank of brigadier general. With General James Polk then serving at the Pentagon and therefore in a position to recommend him, Aaron felt he might be fortunate enough to win the promotion, but there was no way to know for sure.

Janet Ann had made it clear she didn't want to be an officer's wife any longer, and the Cohn children were young and firmly rooted in their home town. It seemed to Aaron that tearing them away from Columbus in their teen and early adult years would be asking too much of them. So, after twenty-five years as a soldier, Aaron had made the heart-breaking decision to retire from the army. For the rest of his life, he would second-guess himself. "I'll always wonder if I'd have gotten that promotion," he often says.

Although he left active service, Aaron stayed in touch with his army friends including his hero, General James Polk. In 1978 Polk commanded USAREUR (US Army, Europe) as a four-star general in Versailles. When a young lieutenant from Luxembourg came to Polk's office to pay his respects, Polk asked him what city he hailed from.

"Bettembourg, sir," replied the young man.

"Bettembourg!" said the general. "Why, your mayor owes me a party." Polk reminded him that his task force had liberated his city in 1944, and before the city could organize a celebration in their honor, the Americans had been ordered to move out toward their next objective.

After meeting General Polk the lieutenant returned to Bettembourg and told his mayor about his encounter with the American liberator. The mayor had been a boy during the war, but he often hoped that someday he would be able to thank personally the Americans who saved his city. The mayor decided to make good the 1944 promise to Polk, and the city began planning a grand celebration to properly acknowledge the Americans' contribution.

As soon as Polk received the invitation he called Aaron,

his former combat operations and planning officer, to ask that Aaron and Janet Ann join him and his family in Luxembourg. Aaron protested. Surely Polk would rather be accompanied by a more high-ranking officer than he.

"Why me?" he asked Polk.

"Because you helped make me a general," Polk said.

The September 1978 festivities commemorating Bettembourg's liberation thirty-four years earlier continued for several days and included a parade with marching bands featuring Polk and Cohn riding in a vintage half-track while crowds shouted to them, "We love you!"

They were honored guests at a flyover, a grand dinner, and a ceremony renaming a thoroughfare the "Rue J. H. Polk." The city of Bettembourg also cited Aaron Cohn for his service in the liberation of Luxembourg.

For Aaron, the highlight of the weekend was a culminating service at the city cathedral. When a band played the Star Spangled Banner in this grand setting, he could have burst with pride for his association with the 3d Armored Cavalry. Aaron returned from Europe with a renewed fervor of nationalism and a stronger reverence for his CO, General Polk.

Other recognitions of Aaron's wartime service followed. In 1982 the US Holocaust Memorial Council honored Aaron as an official liberator of the Ebensee Concentration Camp. Cohn spoke for other liberators when he addressed Gov. Zell Miller, Atlanta Mayor Andrew Young, and other distinguished guests, saying, "We who served in the defense of our great country to fight our enemies during those trying days were privileged to wear the uniform of the greatest country that has ever existed or will ever exist on this earth, and we would do it all over again if it became necessary . . . The lesson which we have all learned at great cost from the holocaust is that no man is an island unto himself. That as Americans we can never stand aside and let any segment of our society, regardless of race, creed, or color, be oppressed for in doing so, we destroy the very fabric of democracy that we all revere, cherish and love so well. And so to all of you we say,

'God Bless America.'"

As the fiftieth anniversary of World War II approached, a number of oral history projects began collecting interviews from witnesses of the holocaust. Judge Cohn eagerly accepted invitations to be interviewed by the Holocaust Memorial Museum in Washington and Emory University's "Witness to the Holocaust" Project.

In 1994 Steven Spielberg, after filming "Schindler's List," established a visual history foundation called "Survivors of the Shoah" (meaning Holocaust). The foundation intended to videotape and archive the interviews of survivors and other witnesses of the Holocaust before the last witnesses to those horrors had passed on. Cohn was among those who were videotaped, and Spielberg acknowledged Aaron's contribution. "Thank you," said Spielberg, "for your invaluable contribution, your strength, and your generosity of spirit."

Gail Cohn and her husband Alex, who was a holocaust survivor himself, traveled to Israel not long after Emory University's oral history holocaust project began collecting testimony. Their tour guide in Jerusalem was another survivor by the name of Eliezer Ayalon. When Ayalon mentioned he had been at Ebensee as a child, Gail told him her father had been a liberator there. Alex sent Ayalon a transcript of Aaron's interview. A few years later Leslie Cohn and his wife Bonnie were visiting Israel when they chanced to have the same tour guide whom Gail and Alex had met. When Leslie learned that Eliezer had been a survivor of Ebensee, Leslie deduced that this was the same man his sister had met.

In 1993 Ayalon came to Columbus to thank Aaron for saving his life and the others of Ebensee. Headlines in the Columbus newspaper proclaimed that the two men had met, talked of their common experiences, and become fast friends. Their meeting was in Ayalon's words "B'shert," a Yiddish word meaning destiny. The two families stayed in touch, and after Ayalon published a book about his experiences as victim of the Nazis, he asked Aaron to write a quote for the cover. Aaron's blurb, printed just

Eliezer Ayalon, who had been a prisoner at Ebensee when Aaron's army
unit liberated it, traveled from Israel to Columbus in 1993 to meet his
liberator.

beneath Elie Wiesel's, stated that Ayalon's story represented "a
true and great saga of the indomitable will to survive in a world
of horror and terror."

In 1985 Aaron Cohn had long passed the normal age of
retirement. He had been serving the families of Muscogee County
for twenty years, and he was sixty-nine years old. Some assumed
he'd be stepping down soon, and perhaps it was partly due to that
assumption that both houses of the Georgia legislature passed
resolutions honoring and commending him for his distinguished
service to the state, and the University of Georgia awarded him
the Distinguished Alumni Merit Award. He also won the "Book
of Golden Deeds Award" from the Columbus Exchange Club.

But Cohn had no intention of leaving the very work that gave
his life meaning. Even though the times were getting meaner and
Cohn's cases now routinely involved guns, drugs, and felonies,

he still loved rising early each day to head to court. Like a Sam Cohn mule in harness he was happiest when pulling his load.

Honors continued to flow his way. In 1987 the American Criminal Justice Association gave him the Julie Lathrop Award for outstanding contributions to the juvenile justice system. On May 10, 1988, Mayor James Jernigan proclaimed the day to be "Judge Aaron Cohn Day" to commemorate his twenty-third year as a juvenile court judge. Journalist Tim Chitwood noted that Cohn "stood to one side as a lineup of state and local officials took turns singing his praises, and he looked just a little uncomfortable at all the adulation being poured upon him."

After the ceremony at the government center party to honor the seventy-two-year-old judge and show off the juvenile court's "new and expanded facilities," Chitwood talked to some of the people who had gathered to honor him. One police officer said, "To me, Aaron Cohn *is* the juvenile court." A school principal said, "He's the best friend a troubled youngster in this town ever had." And a minister told the journalist about the day he witnessed a custody case involving three children. The father was a college chum of Cohn's and had a "high-priced lawyer" and lots of money, while the mother and her new husband were not rich and not well known. "The judge decided the children should stay with their mother. No show of wealth, fancy legal footwork, or college ties tangled his judgment. That was a powerful example of a man who will do what's right," said the minister. "He's going to do what's right—no matter who it offends, who's happy, or who's sad . . . That takes guts."

After talking to the crowd, Chitwood pressed the judge on whether he was going to retire soon. Cohn said there was nothing magic about the number seventy and that he intended to work for many years to come. He had reached the pinnacle of power and respect as a juvenile court judge, with local, state, and national recognition for his dedication to America's children.

"I owe Columbus," he told the reporter. "And I don't think you pay your debts by just paying taxes."

Nine days later the Muscogee County Department of

Family and Children Services honored him for his many years of dedicated service to the children of Muscogee County, Georgia. In 1988 the Columbus Chapter of the Child Abuse Council honored him with the "Aaron Cohn Humanitarian Award" for his work with abused and neglected children.

In 1989 the National Council of Juvenile and Family Court Judges awarded him the Meritorious Service Award to the Juvenile Courts of America. A few months later the State Bar of Georgia recognized his accomplishments to the state by resolution, and the Columbus Bar Association presented him with the "Liberty Bell Award."

In 1990 two more awards came his way as the local boy scouts presented him with the "Outstanding Citizen of Columbus" award, and the Georgia Criminal Justice Council gave him the

Georgia Governor Joe Frank Harris awards Cohn with the Governor's Criminal Justice Coordinating Council Leadership Award in 1990.

In 1987 Judge Cohn won the Julie Lathrop Award for outstanding contributions to the juvenile justice system.

Governor's Leadership Award for his work in juvenile justice.

Then in December 1995 Carpenter's Way (a haven for trouble boys created by retired major league baseball player Glen Davis) named Cohn the recipient of their first humanitarian award, which would forever after be known as the "Judge Aaron Cohn Humanitarian Award." And in 1996 the Columbus Chamber of Commerce honored Cohn with the "James W. Woodruff Jr. Memorial Award" for his "continuous service to humankind." This recognition was considered to be "the highest honor that may be bestowed on a citizen of Columbus for lifetime commitment to community service."

The judge also was appointed to serve as a charter member of the Chattahoochee Valley Sports Hall of Fame nominations committee for athletes. In January 1997 the Family Center of Columbus honored Cohn with their very first award given to an individual for strengthening families in the Columbus community—the Family Championship Award.

Two more distinctions came to him in 1998. Aaron received the local Congressional Medal of Honor Society Commendation for public and patriotic service, and the Rotary Club of Columbus presented him with the International Award of the Paul Harris Fellowship. And in 1999, the University of Georgia Law School awarded Cohn and Governor Roy Barnes with the Distinguished Service Scroll Award, its highest honor.

All the years Aaron Cohn had quietly worked for the children and families of his home town without expecting or receiving any acknowledgment were now behind him. For decades he had told his children, "you get out of a community what you put into it." The proof of that now gleamed on his wall.

While these honors meant a great deal to the judge, he kept his nose to the grindstone. The typical crimes in his caseload were becoming more serious. Nationally, such juvenile crimes as murder and school shootings led to a public outcry for punishment at the same level as adult perpetrators, and yet the juvenile court remained a predominantly rehabilitative court, and Cohn believed it should stay that way.

His most effective tactic for turning lives around remained scaring the daylights out of the minors who came before him while also giving them every break he could. His words of wisdom rang so true that delinquents and parents alike awoke from their complacency by such no-nonsense directives as, "Look in the mirror and you'll see your own worst enemy."

He told the mother of a car thief, "You son doesn't need cars. He needs an education!"

Occasionally angry delinquents defied the judge, even threatening violence. On one occasion an enraged teenager lunged at Judge Cohn. The bailiffs pounced on him and held him back, but the surprising part of the scene was that the judge just sat there glowering at the boy as he charged toward him instead of leaving the court room as security policy dictated.

Later, when someone asked him why he had not vacated

the room, Cohn sneered, "I fought in the damn Battle of the Bulge! I'm not leaving my court room."

On another occasion, a delinquent blasted the judge with epithets of his own.

"F____ you!" the child screamed at the judge after sentencing.

The teenager's mortified mother tore out of the gallery, ripped off her shoe, and began drilling the kid over the head with the heel of it.

"Ma'am," said the judge slowly and calmly as the frailing continued. "I can't allow you to do that."

But before the bailiff (moving uncharacteristically slowly) stopped her, she was able to get in a dozen more licks.

For all the wrath the judge demonstrated in court, as soon as he stepped down from the bench Aaron Cohn transformed into a soft-spoken, gentle man who doted on his family, employees, and friends. He told those close to him he had not intended to grow up to become the town boogey man, but if that's what it took to turn the children of southwest Georgia toward the straight and narrow, he was glad to do it.

Even though he is known to wayward youth as "the scary judge," he also is reputed to be fair. One policeman commented, "A kid can't go to juvenile court and say he didn't get a break." Judge Cohn sentenced a second-time offender to probation one December after seeing that the child's parents and entire family had appeared in court for the first time. Convinced they were now taking their son's behavior seriously and forgetting that the child was not a Christian, the judge told the boy he was giving him an early Christmas present. Afterward, in the judge's chambers, a representative of the DA's office said, "Well, wasn't that something? A Jewish judge gave an early Christmas present to a Muslim kid."

Aaron smiled and said, "Only in America."

In January 2000 Aaron came to the difficult decision to close his law practice. He had been spending more and more time at court, and he hated not to pull his weight in his partnership with

Leslie. When the state offered him a "full-time" salary, he felt he finally had the liberty of focusing only on one thing, even though he actually experienced a decrease in income. Money never had been as important to the judge as job fulfillment, and settling down to one line of work was a great relief.

In 2002 the superior court judges created the Chattahoochee Judicial Circuit Juvenile Court to include five other counties. Cohn became the presiding judge of it with two associate judges (Warner Kennon and Wayne Jernigan Sr.) sharing an enlarged geographic area, extending as far as Butler, Georgia, sixty miles away.

The designation also marked another personal milestone. With thirty-seven years of service behind him, the eighty-six-year-old Aaron Cohn became the longest-sitting juvenile court judge in America, and an editorial in the local newspaper noted that "with Judge Cohn at the helm, [the new judicial circuit] could hardly be in better hands."

Honors continued to pour in. On May 27, 2003, Congressman Sanford D. Bishop Jr. presented Cohn with a "Certificate of Special Congressional Recognition" for outstanding achievement, service, and distinction. On this same day Gen. Barry McCaffrey, a hero of the 1991 Persian Gulf War, presented Cohn with the "Livingston Citizen-Soldier of the Year" award by the Association of the US Army for his wartime contributions as well as his community service since returning from service in Europe.

In November 2003 the Georgia Council of Juvenile Court Judges hosted a banquet in Judge Cohn's honor to celebrate his nearly forty years of service to the juvenile courts of Georgia. He also received the "Amicus Curiae" Award from the Georgia Supreme Court and resolutions from the Georgia Court of Appeals and the Superior Court of the Chattahoochee Judicial Circuit. And in 2004 Cohn accepted the Golden Service and Leadership Award for "over fifty years of dedicated and faithful service to Temple Israel."

By this time the detention center on Schatulga Road that Judge Cohn had worked so hard to build over thirty years before had long since become outgrown and outmoded. After years of trying to persuade legislators to fund a new pre-adjudication center, he and others finally succeeded. The new state-of-the-art facility off Macon Road, dedicated in 2004, held over twice as many youth (eighty) as had the former center next door. Together with its neighboring institution, the Muscogee Youth Detention Center, the complex encompassed over sixty thousand square feet of residential, educational, medical, recreational, and administrative spaces.

Perhaps Aaron should not have been surprised when the General Assembly voted to name the new facility the "Aaron Cohn Regional Youth Detention Center," but he was—surprised and delighted.

When he stood before the assembled crowd at the dedication ceremony in October 2005 Judge Cohn was a forty-year veteran of the juvenile court bench. Georgia Department of Juvenile Justice Commissioner Albert Murray remarked, "Judge Cohn is a living example of what serving our fellow man really means and a living example of the spirit of America . . . It is my hope that the youth who leave this facility will follow in his great footsteps."

With Janet Ann at his side, Judge Cohn told the audience, "It is a blessing to be

In 2004 the state legislature voted to name the new regional detention center after Aaron.

Janet Ann stands with Aaron as he is honored at the opening of the
Aaron Cohn Regional Youth Detention Center in 2005.

acknowledged while one is still alive to see it." After all, he was
eighty-nine years old.

But to understand just how precious this honor was to him,
one had only to look at the framed, quotation by an unknown
author, which had been setting on his desk for many years.

His touchstone read, "A hundred years from now it will not
matter what my bank account was, the sort of house I live in, or
the kind of car I drive. But the world may be different because I
was important in the life of a child."

CHAPTER 14

THE HONORABLE AARON COHN

To quote Jane Cohn Kulbersh, Aaron Cohn has "grown old with grace and focus." This focus his daughter speaks of has been fixed like a junkyard dog on the things that matter most to him—his family, his community, his university, his nation, and his profession.

Today citations and awards compete for space along the walls of his den and office and on his crowded trophy shelves. Having lived in and loved Columbus, Georgia, for over ninety years, the judge is now a local institution. In fact, it is difficult to find a Columbus citizen who has not been encouraged, inspired, protected, or disciplined by him. He is, as Gene Asher, the author of *Legends: Georgians Who Lived Impossible Dreams*, has written, "perhaps Columbus's most beloved citizen."

In 2007 his home town recognized the judge for his forty-three years of service in the juvenile court with a ceremony on the courthouse steps in which the mayor noted that Cohn was the city's oldest and longest-serving employee. Seated in the crowd that day was a surprise guest, Jubilate Sack, who had been the teenaged niece of Bino Siedhof, the celebrated German tennis coach whose family the young Major Aaron Cohn befriended and defended in the aftermath of World War II. To Jubilate and her family, Cohn had been "not a conqueror, but a humanitarian,"

Judge Cohn offers advice on rearing children to the *Valley Parent* magazine.

and so she felt privileged to be able to personally express her gratitude and adoration once more.

Within months of the courthouse ceremony an African American church feted Cohn with a banquet and presented him with another humanitarian award. A magazine featured his words of wisdom in an article entitled "Judge Cohn's Simple Truths" which offered such down-to-earth parenting guidelines as "Take charge or lose control."

Even with all the honors he has received of late, Aaron still has no intention of resting on these laurels. Today as yesterday, Judge Cohn scares the living daylights out of the minors who appear in his courtroom. He tells them, "So you don't want people telling you what to do? Let me tell you something. All my life people have told me what to do. I am ninety-two years old, and people are still expecting me to do the right thing, so get over it."

Yes, Aaron Cohn is still doing the right thing. A few years ago, Aaron asked his son Leslie to drive him to a funeral.

"Why are you going to *his* funeral?" Leslie asked.

"Our families were close. It's the right thing to do."

At the graveside service, they were both surprised to see that a crowd of people had come, even though the man was not well liked. Aaron leaned close to Leslie's ear and said, "You know, people come to funerals for two reason. First of all, they come to pay their respects to the family. And secondly, they come to make sure the SOB is put in the ground."

Today Judge Cohn often is thanked for making those hard decisions in court that brought wayward children to the brink of a reckoning. Dozens of them tell him today, "Even though I was angry at you at the time, you did the right thing." He encounters people wherever he goes who tell him that he was responsible for turning their lives around. One young man showed up in the judge's chambers on Christmas Eve just to give him a hug and a personal thank you.

"I gave you a lot of trouble," he said, "but you never gave up on me."

Recently Aaron and his son Leslie were sitting in Aaron's favorite barbecue restaurant, Smokey Pig, when a big, scowling

Aaron Cohn, third from left, was inducted into the Chattahoochee Valley Sports Hall of Fame in 2007 for his tennis accomplishments.

man with tattoos emblazoned on both arms walked through the door and straight toward Aaron. Both Aaron and Leslie (who is no spring chicken at the age of sixty-one) steeled themselves for what looked like a fight.

The man stopped right in front of Aaron; he looked down on the elder and asked, "Are you Judge Cohn?"

Belying the pang of fear in his gut, Aaron swelled to his full height—a height that had slightly diminished with the passing of time. Aaron looked the stranger right in the eye. "Yes, I am," he declared.

"Do you know what you did?" asked the man, and Leslie balled his fists, ready for a fight. The stranger pointed through the window to a pick up truck in the parking lot.

"You see that truck over there?"

Aaron said yes, not knowing where in the world the conversation was going.

"You see that name on the truck? Well, that's my truck and my business name on it. Years ago I was heading for trouble, and you gave me a chance."

The burly man clutched the surprised judge in a bear hug. With a beaming smile he said, "Thank you for believing in me."

The judge's most recent honor came in June 2008 when he was tapped to receive the Georgia Bar's Tradition of Excellence Award, one of the most prestigious awards a member of the judiciary can receive. Only one judge per year is so honored, and never before had a seated juvenile judge been chosen. To Aaron's mind, this proved that society was beginning to value its children. In accepting the award, Cohn told a humorous story to illustrate just how long he had been employed as a juvenile court judge.

"In 1965 I enjoyed sharing a program in Columbus with a very friendly peanut farmer who was then a state senator. At that time I was judge of the Juvenile Court of Muscogee County, Georgia, and we had a delightful program. Later this state senator became governor of our great state, and I was still judge of the Juvenile Court of Muscogee County, Georgia. In time, he became President of the United States of America, and I was still judge of the Juvenile Court of Muscogee County, Georgia. Today, he no longer has his position, but I still have mine."

Like that aging peanut farmer, Aaron has the life force of someone half his age. When his wife Janet Ann encourages him to take a nap, he tells her, "As long as I'm living, I'm gonna get up and live. There's plenty of time to sleep later." Perhaps it is that very determination to live life so fully that led to the *Columbus Ledger-Enquirer*'s including him among the city's "one hundred citizens to remember during the twentieth century."

With the joie de vivre of a six-year-old on summer vacation, the judge bounds out of bed each day. Coworkers often hear him singing silly nonsense songs as he pads down the courthouse halls.

"I didn't steal that pork chop. That pork chop followed me home."

The only thing in life he will not tolerate without complaint is being served a flat Diet Coke.

Cohn adores any and all holidays, and he looks forward to hosting the Christmas office party each year. He is forever asking employees how he can help them, and as Carolyn Hester, his courtroom coordinator, says, "His name is like a key. It opens doors."

In all his years in the public eye, the most hot water he ever got himself into was the time he called a northern reporter "sugar." He now knows he's being politically incorrect when he does this, but he can't help himself. He loves being surrounded by women, and there is always a bevy of them at his beck and call, from court employees to household and personal assistants. He only wishes he had gotten this much attention from the gentler sex when he was younger.

Although he no longer plays tennis, recognitions of his more active days continue to roll in. Columbus State University bestowed on him an honorary doctorate of humane letters for his long service on the university athletics board. In 2001 the Columbus Regional Tennis Association created an award

The UGA scoreboard illumines the visage of the Honorable Aaron Cohn as he receives the Bill Hartman Award in 2005.

in his name to be given to "the most deserving juvenile for sportsmanship." In 2006 his alma mater awarded him the Old Faithful Dawg award at a halftime ceremony. And in 2007 the judge was inducted as a member of the elite Chattahoochee Valley Sports Hall of Fame for his accomplishments in tennis.

Winning the University of Georgia's Bill Hartman Award in 2005 was his most prized athletic accomplishment. This award, named for Aaron's childhood chum who played ball with him on the lawn of the Muscogee County Courthouse before becoming a professional football player, recognizes former UGA student-athletes who demonstrate twenty or more years of excellence in their profession.

Sadly, Bill Hartman died not long afterwards, but the fact that Cohn received this award during half time of Georgia's homecoming game made the moment that much sweeter. With his wife, his children, and a few of his grandchildren there to cheer him on that crisp October day, Judge Cohn stood once again on Sanford Stadium's fifty yard line. The scoreboard broadcast his bigger-than-life image to the packed stands while below his picture blinked the title "The Honorable Judge Aaron Cohn."

That golden moment on the gridiron highlighted his unwavering passion for his university and his life long love affair with sports. Few people have loved University of Georgia sports as passionately and as long as has Judge Cohn. Just as when he was six and he stood on the dusty roadside near the Columbus Memorial Stadium after a Georgia-Auburn game to ask "Who beat?" Aaron still grows glum when Georgia loses a game in any sport.

Since 1953 when Cohn bought his first set of football season tickets, he has not missed a home game except on the few dates that fell on a High Holy Day. When his

The Miracle in the City Foundation recognition was one of Cohn's many recent honors.

In 2008 Judge Cohn was honored with the Georgia Bar's
highest recognition for a judge, the "Tradition of Excellence
Award." Photo is courtesy of the *Georgia Bar Journal.*

godson announced he was getting married on the same date as a
UGA home game, Aaron called him to say, "I really want to be
at your wedding, so you'll need to change the date." (He did.)

Today as Aaron mounts the endless stadium steps to reach
his seat on the final row of Sanford Stadium—a seat he has kept
for over forty years because he is too superstitious to change it—
he sets his jaw in determination. With virtually no cartilage left
in his knees, the foray is torturous, but there is no place on Earth
he would rather be on a Saturday afternoon in autumn than in
Athens, Georgia, cheering on his team.

Recently, on his ninety-second birthday Aaron was thrilled
to see every member of his large, extended family gather in
Columbus from all over the Southeast. But he was equally happy
when they left in time for him to rush to Auburn, Alabama, to
watch the Georgia tennis team compete.

After fifty years of living in their family home on Preston
Drive, Aaron and Janet Ann decided it was time to think about
scaling down and moving to an upscale, new retirement complex
on the edge of town. But as soon as Aaron had paid down his
money, he regretted it. He called his son Leslie and said, "You're
my lawyer. Get my money back." When Leslie succeeded, Aaron
was thrilled at the prospect of spending the rest of his days in the

home he had built for his family—a family that now spans four generations and includes seven grandchildren and nine great grandchildren. Aaron's enthusiasm for UGA sports has spread to his two sons-in-law, Harvey Danits and David Kulbersh, and he's proud that his daughter-in-law, Bonnie, is as loyal a mother to her children as Aaron's mother was to him.

Although the Cohn family now is scattered over three states, they remain as close as when they all lived on the same floor of their multi-storied home. The household telephone rings frequently as caring loved ones check in. Following in the footsteps of their patriarch, most of Aaron and Janet Ann's children and grandchildren went on to graduate from the University of Georgia, and all have become leaders in their respective cities, having learned well the credo of their forefathers' faith to give back to one's community.

Like their "Poppy" once did, the grandchildren enjoy coaching their children's sports teams, and among Aaron's descendants are a couple of doctors, an attorney who advocates for children with learning disabilities, a teacher, and a sports and recreation director. Put these professions together, and you have yourself a Techni-colored version of Aaron Cohn.

Loyal friends like Dan Magill, who coached UGA's tennis team for several decades and whom Aaron considers to be "the best Bulldog ever," have championed Aaron since the days they competed in the state YMCA table tennis championship back in 1933. In a recent *Athens Banner-Herald* column, Magill wrote that Aaron is now the University's oldest tennis letterman. The article showered compliments on Cohn, but Aaron was touched most by the closing line, which sums up what is most important to the judge after a long life of public and private victories.

"Cohn," said Magill, "is a great American."

All that Aaron Cohn has ever aspired to do was to live up to the standards his parents idealized as being thoroughly American—being fair, courageous, competitive, willing to take unpopular stands for the betterment of all, and to be a champion of those who need a champion most. Having sacrificed much, he now has seen the rewards of a near-century of life lived with courage, commitment and compassion.

Born a first-generation American, Aaron has weathered prejudice and bigotry to become, in Dr. Tommy Lawhorne's words, "a paragon of dignity and character . . . and a damn good Dawg."

Aaron Cohn is, indeed, a great American.

Endnotes

1 Remembrance of Frank Jeziorski in, *The 150 Year Saga of The 3rd U.S. Cavalry,* (Ft. Carson, CO: 3rd Armored Cavalry Regiment, 1996), 5.

2 *The 150 Year Saga,* 9.

3 Ibid., 63. Joe Radanovich was a favorite of Aaron Cohn's. An original inductee at Camp Gordon, Joe was very helpful to Cohn while a Squadron S-3.

4 L. VanLoan Naisawald, "Odyssey of the Colors: A Cold War Drama," *American History Illustrated,* Vol. 1, No. 9, January 1967, 34-41.

5 Hereinafter, the words of James H. Polk come from his memoir, *World War II Letters and Notes of Colonel James H. Polk,* (Oakland, OR: Red Anvil Press, 2005).

6 By the new code, Corps command was designated Comet, and the 3d Cavalry was referred to as Cowhand. Following that designation, each regimental officer used a number to designate their position on the staff. For instance, Aaron, as S-3, was "Cowhand 3."

7 Maj. Aaron Cohn, "A Cavalry Task Force in the Defense of a River Line," *Cavalry Journal,* July/August 1945, 28.

8 Ibid., 29.

9 *The 150 Year Saga,* 127.

10 Ibid., 161.

11 Neile Sue Friedman, *A Cup of Honey: The Story of a Young Holocaust Survivor, Eliezer Ayalon,* (Friedman & Ayalon, 1999), 187.

12 Dr. Michael Marunchak, "Dying and Living in Ebensee: Recollections of Prisoner No. 120482, found at http://www.ukrweekly.com/Archive/2002/180218.shtml, March 1, 2004.

13 Ibid.

14 Letter of Capt. Tim Brennan, F Company, 3rd Squadron, printed in *The 150 Year Saga,* 194.

The Cohn family celebrates Aaron's 90th birthday.

Aaron and Janet Ann Cohn,
a.k.a. "Poppy and Grand Nanna,"

Wish to express their love and gratitude for

Their children:

Gail Cohn and Harvey Danits
Leslie and Bonnie Cohn
Jane and David Kulbersh

Their grandchildren:

Melissa Danits
Howie and Kim Rosenberg
David and Sheri Rosenberg
Eliot Rosenberg
Al and Tracy Cohn
Seth Cohn
Leslie and Aaron Lipson
Jonathan Kulbersh

And their great grandchildren:

Evan, Noah, Aaron, Jonah,
Morgan, Abby, Lexi, Karen & Rory

1556809

Made in the USA